T0121551

HEAT and LIGHT

HEAT and LIGHT

Advice for the Next Generation of Journalists

MIKE WALLACE
and
BETH KNOBEL

THREE RIVERS PRESS • NEW YORK

Published in the United States by Three Rivers Press, an imprint of the Crown Publishing Group, a division of Random House, Inc., New York.
www.crownpublishing.com

Three Rivers Press and the Tugboat design are registered trademarks of Random House, Inc.

Library of Congress Cataloging-in-Publication Data

Wallace, Mike, 1918–
Heat and light / Mike Wallace and Beth Knobel.—1st ed.
p. cm.
1. Journalism. 2. Broadcast journalism. 3. Journalism—Vocational guidance. I. Knobel, Beth. II. Title.
PN4775.W215 2010
070.4—dc22 2009052613

ISBN 978-0-307-46465-1

Design by Helene Berinsky

First Edition

146122990

To Chris

and

to Alex

Contents

HEAT and LIGHT

INTRODUCTION

A journalist is a grumbler, a censurer,
a giver of advice, a regent of sovereigns, a tutor
of nations. Four hostile newspapers are more
to be feared than a thousand bayonets.

—NAPOLEON BONAPARTE, French leader

Our View of Journalism

This is a book about how to create good journalism, and perhaps even great journalism. One author, Mike Wallace, is one of America's premier journalists, with almost seventy years of experience as a reporter and anchorman. He has won nearly every prize a television journalist can receive, including twenty-one Emmy Awards, most of them for his work on CBS News' *60 Minutes*. The other author, Beth Knobel, is an award-winning reporter turned journalism educator whose experience in newspapers, radio, and television stretches back nearly thirty years. The journalist and the journalism professor are teaming up in this book to unlock the mysteries of our profession, in the hope that our stories and advice will be useful to the next generation of journalists.

In doing so, we realize that this is a particularly difficult time to be starting out in journalism. As we write this, the news business is in terrible shape. Newspapers and magazines are folding in droves as their costs start to outstrip their revenues. Almost every print publication is shrinking, because fewer and fewer readers are willing to pay for something they can get for free on the Internet. Network television, too, is attracting fewer and fewer viewers to its news programs. Not only are there few new jobs in traditional journalism these days, but the number of jobs overall has continued to fall—thousands of journalists have lost their jobs in recent months. This creates an extremely difficult situation for all reporters, but for young journalists in particular.

This state of affairs makes the need for this book *more* urgent, not less. Young journalists will need all the knowledge and skills they can get to compete in this tough market. Journalists who are starting out will need to show that they know the best practices in the business, in terms of both skills and knowledge. And even as the media landscape changes and the Internet comes to dominate other media, the journalists who will be working in the twenty-first century will benefit from the fundamentals we recommend in this book. The medium may change, but the essentials of quality journalism remain the same. "Adapting to change will challenge us all," says Marcus Brauchli, executive editor of the *Washington Post*. "But the fundamentals of journalism will continue to matter whatever shape the new information ecosystem takes."

As much as the media landscape may be changing, there will always be a need for good journalism. It's one of the pillars on which our country has been built. The founding fathers knew it. "Were it left to me to decide whether we should have a government without newspapers or newspapers without a government, I should not hesitate a moment to prefer the latter," Thomas Jefferson said all the way back in 1787. And today's leaders know it. "Your ultimate success as an industry is essential to the success of our democracy," President Obama declared at the 2009 White House Correspondents' Dinner, addressing a roomful of the country's top journalists. "You help all of us who serve at the pleasure of the American people do our jobs better by holding us accountable, by demanding honesty, by preventing us from taking shortcuts and falling into easy political games that people are so desperately weary of."

You can point to literally millions of examples of courageous journalists uncovering wrongdoing, bringing useful news into the public eye, or otherwise changing lives for the better. The father of American broadcast journalism, the CBS News correspondent Edward R. Murrow, helped bring down a senator who was destroying innocent people's lives by accusing them of being communists. He exposed and tried to end the exploitation of underpaid farm workers. He lobbied for civil rights. The late, great Walter Cronkite, whom we'll discuss later in the book, effectively helped to end the Vietnam War when he said, after a reporting trip there in 1968, that the war was unwinnable. Just a few years later, two metro reporters at the *Washington Post* covered a little break-in at the Democratic National Committee headquarters at the Watergate Hotel, and the ensuing story brought down a president. These are a few of the larger moments of American journalism history, yet smaller but still crucially important stories are broken every single day. Multiply that by every country in the world and you get an idea of how important the press can be.

Despite the current economic challenges, history suggests that journalism is unlikely to disappear. During the past hundred years or so, every time a new communications medium has been introduced, people thought it would destroy journalism. When radio first became a mass medium, people thought it would kill off good newspaper reporting. When television came along, people thought it would make both newspapers and radio obsolete. Now, with the changes being wrought by the Internet, many people wonder if journalism can survive. We are absolutely certain that it can. And it must. The fact that applications to journalism schools and programs are increasing tells us that young people haven't yet been scared off.

Still, each of those paradigm shifts presented new challenges for journalists, and the period we're living through is no exception. The problems journalism now faces aren't just financial—they're structural. The Internet makes it easy to disseminate information, but it doesn't necessarily make the information disseminated true or trustworthy. The Internet makes it all too easy to rewrite existing articles instead of doing original work. With the advent of blogging, people's own musings sometimes take precedence over real reporting. In all forms of media, gossip is often being reported as fact, and substance sometimes takes a backseat to sensation. The overall discourse has become shorter and more superficial.

Although Mike and Beth are two generations apart, our view of journalism is essentially the same. We both see journalism as a tool to educate, not just titillate. We both think that journalists have to break new ground in order to have done their job right. We both think that journalists have a responsibility to tell their audience what they *need* to know, not just what they *want* to know. We both think journalists have a special responsibility, more than ever before, to help people make sense of complicated and controversial issues.

These statements may sound self-evident to anyone who's ever worked as a reporter or editor, but our rather old-fashioned view of journalism is worth emphasizing in today's climate. In these pages, we'll try to explain to young journalists how to create what we consider to be great journalism—reports with both dramatic heat and informational light. That is to say, we hope to explain how to create journalism that is not just dramatic but also informed, knowledgeable, and groundbreaking—like the journalism we've aspired to create in our careers.

What we've tried to do here is to produce a book that explains the profession of journalism to students and young reporters, but which isn't a textbook. Textbooks, while instructive, are difficult to sit down and read. Journalism needs a manifesto right now to set young journalists on the right path, and we hope that this is it.

We hope that the stories, lessons, and thoughts contained in these pages will help inspire young journalists to carry the torch as it should be carried—and give them the basic skills they need to get started. We cannot say that we know everything there is to know about this profession, or that we've always been perfect journalists ourselves. But our decades of work and those of our friends have provided some good stories and useful lessons.

Journalism will kill you, but it will keep you alive while you're at it.

—HORACE GREELEY, newspaper editor

Why This Book?

This work was born at Fordham University in New York in late 2007, where Beth teaches a class entitled "Television News Innovators." Mike is one of these innovators, and he agreed to speak to Beth's students for the same reason he sat down to work on this book: he is anxious to do what he can to pass along his wealth of experience to the next generation.

Mike and Beth had met years earlier when they were colleagues at CBS. Before coming to Fordham, Beth had worked for CBS News, serving as the Moscow bureau chief from 1999 to 2006 and as a Moscow-based producer for two years before that. Mike and Beth had worked together on two stories in Moscow, during which we shared a few meals and a few laughs, and we'd kept in touch on all things Russian.

Many of Beth's students later called Mike's appearance at Fordham awe-inspiring. Simply put, he Mike Wallaced them—that is to say, he started questioning *them* instead of the other way around. After taking some questions that day, Mike started walking up to students and interrogating them, asking them what they thought of television news and of their Fordham education. "How many of you get your news from the Internet?" he asked. "How many of you watch CNN?" And the questions quickly escalated into questions of life and death. "Where do you go when you die? Is there a heaven?" Mike asked of the two hundred students who came to hear him. "Or do we just crumple?" The questions were very relevant to Mike, who was eighty-nine at the time. At first, the students seemed too stunned to talk, but they eventually opened up.

Beth realized that Mike had touched a nerve with her students that day. And several of Beth's colleagues were also moved by Mike's words. Paul Levinson, then chair of the Fordham Department of Communication and Media Studies, praised Mike's appearance on his blog, "Infinite Regress": "[Wallace's] most significant moments at Fordham today came when he effortlessly moved from his role as guest lecturer to his much more familiar role as astute questioner," wrote Levinson. "It was quite extraordinary. And deeply appropriate. What is a reporter, an investigative journalist, after all, if not a teacher, and sometimes of the most profound things, to the public at large." Those comments gave Beth an idea about how to tap in to Mike's natural abilities as a teacher, as well as her own, and she suggested they collaborate on a book. Much to her delight, Mike liked the idea.

So starting in December 2007 we met at Mike's home in Manhattan on a regular basis to discuss the meaning of journalism. Beth made a list of the one hundred or so most basic questions her students ask her, and then we set out to try to answer them. Some of them were sweeping, like "What is good journalism?" or "What is objectivity?" Some were specific: "When you walk into a room to do an interview, what's the first thing you do?" We also watched some of Mike's work for inspiration.

Mike has already written two volumes of memoirs, *Close Encounters* (with Gary Paul Gates; William Morrow, 1987) and *Between You and Me* (with Gary Paul Gates; Hyperion, 2005), which cover the bulk of his career. But those books do not cover the essentials of the practice of journalism. Neither of those books answers the questions that Mike knows so much about—say, how to interview someone, or what separates good journalism from great journalism. So this book is something different from what Mike has done before. It's a chance for him to pass along the secrets of his remarkable career.

The book tackles many of the large questions behind journalistic work, such as the meaning of truth, objectivity, and ethical behavior, but we also write extensively about the nuts and bolts of putting together a report, including generating story ideas, preparing questions, and writing well. A main focus of the book, given Mike's background, is interviewing. We also muse about the future of journalism.

You'll find that we quote people and examples from CBS News extensively in this book. This is not because CBS is the best network or has the best news operation, but because we're both products of CBS News and have been shaped by its practices and traditions. And many parts of that long and history-filled tradition are worth sharing with young journalists.

Seven chapters will follow this introduction. Chapter 1 covers the essential questions of journalism, including truth, objectivity, the definition of news, and why one should be a journalist. Chapter 2 focuses on the preparation for doing a good story, including the generation of story ideas and deciding whom to interview. Chapter 3 covers the mechanics of interviewing. Chapter 4 focuses on writing a story for print. Chapter 5 covers putting together a story for broadcast or the Internet. Chapter 6 is a primer on ethics and media law. And Chapter 7 covers the future of journalism. We also include a Reporters' Toolbox at the end, where readers can find checklists, suggested readings, activities for further learning, and a list of online resources.

We hope *Heat and Light* will be something that both journalism students and lovers of the news can read to receive a grounding in the profession, and to find the inspiration to do journalism as it should be done.

1

THE FUNDAMENTALS OF GREAT JOURNALISM

The duty of journalists is to tell the truth.
Journalism means you go back to the actual facts,
you look at the documents, you discover what
the record is, and you report it that way.

—NOAM CHOMSKY, professor and author

An old television ad for the U.S. military gushes, "It's not just a job—it's an adventure!" The same might well be said of the profession of journalism. We think it's the best job in the world. It's exciting. It's interesting. It's important. "I cannot think of a more interesting, fulfilling way to spend your life," says Mike. "A reporter's life, by God, it's an absolutely wonderful life. Somebody's paying the bill to educate you—to send you around the world, if you prove worthy."

In this chapter, we'll talk about why it's worth becoming a journalist, and what kind of personality and skills you need to become a journalist. We'll also explain some of the most basic things that journalists must do well, and some basic principles that should guide them. They're the kind of rules that not only guide both of us but also form the foundation for most of America's best-known anchors and reporters.

The Gospel of Journalism

The central goal of journalism is to separate fact from fiction. "Mike has always said that we are seekers of truth, and that's what we are. We are seekers of truths that people would be better off knowing and that they probably don't know," says Mike's longtime producer at *60 Minutes*, Robert Anderson. "And we are looking for something that is hopefully of some significance, because the more significant it is, the better the story it is for us."

Organizations that have consistently been able to uncover those kinds of important stories have become the pillars of American journalism. Consider *60 Minutes*. The show was not an immediate success. When it first started, it was in eighty-sixth place in the ratings. But it became arguably the most successful show ever on television, with ratings in the top ten for more than three decades. The key to its success is not only its exclusivity—that people will see stories there they can get nowhere else—but also because the show digs to the bottom of complicated matters. "Thirty-five million people were watching because they knew that they were getting carefully researched truth. And that's what they were after," Mike explains.

But most of all, journalism is important. Journalists keep politicians honest. They shine a light on injustice. They tell people things that improve the quality of their lives. They keep our society free. "A vibrant press, a free press, is the single best check on the growth of authoritarianism, on the spread of totalitarianism," says Marvin Kalb, former correspondent for CBS News and NBC News, and professor emeritus at Harvard University. "A free press guarantees a free society. That's why it's so terribly important."

Without journalists, government waste and corruption might go unnoticed. Without them, people wouldn't know about important medical advances. And without reporters, we wouldn't know who is in need and how to help them. Simply put, journalists make our world a better place.

Robert Anderson says the stories he's proudest of are the ones that revealed evil or good. One that springs to his mind is a piece he did about a U.S. government program that provides drugs to people in other nations who are living with HIV and AIDS. "Today there are two to three million people alive, most of them in Africa, because of a program that George Bush started, that a bipartisan Congress approved, of providing pills to people with HIV/AIDS. And for years people were dying in Africa from AIDS and Americans didn't really know about it," Anderson explains. His team went off to Uganda and met with people who would have died had they not been provided with medication through this program. "We were pointing out that they're all living because we're providing the pills. I find that an amazingly significant story," he says.

Most journalists say there's a certain sense of responsibility involved in deciding to become a reporter, beyond what you might find in choosing most other professions. The best journalists have a kind of fire in their belly about what they do. "It is a calling. It really is," says Mike. Roger Mudd, the veteran CBS and NBC News correspondent, writes of this feeling in his recent book, *The Place to Be*—a work about the glory days of the CBS Washington bureau, from the early 1960s to the early 1980s. "Most of us thought ourselves chosen. It was as if we had been lifted up by a journalistic deity and dropped down in the middle of the Washington bureau to serve our country by doing God's work," writes Mudd. The best journalists we both know, like Mudd, see themselves as performing a critically important function in seeking to root out the truth. "Exposing evil, exposing impropriety, exposing something that shouldn't be happening, is our highest calling and we do it in hopes that by shining a light on it, the light will purify," says Anderson. "And that's a pretty high calling, as opposed to just trying to fill a page or fill an hour, if you can reveal something and make the world better."

As important as journalism is, it's also *fun*. We think it's about as much fun as any job can be. What could be better than spending your days speaking with interesting people about the world's most compelling issues? Top journalists such as Mike get to meet lots of important people—presidents, writers, and scientists. But he's also interviewed thousands of everyday people, people who had been through something interesting or newsworthy. It's not always the famous people who are the most memorable, says Mike. "It's the people, the characters in history, who have accomplished certain things in certain areas." For example, controversial euthanasia advocate Dr. Jack Kevorkian, whom Mike interviewed in 1998 and 2007, was not an elected official or a television star. He was just a person whose actions turned him into a public figure—a very controversial public figure. Kevorkian kicked up a national debate over assisted suicide by helping several people take their own lives. These were people who were suffering from various diseases, and many of them endured chronic pain. Kevorkian's actions—which eventually landed him in prison—polarized the country. Some people called him an angel of mercy; others dubbed him "Dr. Death." "I had great respect for him. He had the guts to do what he believed was right," says Mike, "and he knew he was going to wind up in trouble because of it." Mike liked covering Kevorkian precisely because the doctor's actions were so controversial. "This is the sort of thing that a reporter loves to get, something that is questioned by everyone because it hits home with everyone," Mike explains.

Most reporters we know have had amazing adventures and

met remarkable people through their work. When Kim Murphy, a Pultizer Prize–winning correspondent for the *Los Angeles Times,* thinks of some of her favorite stories, she says it's not really the big ones or the best ones that come to mind. "Interviewing the mayor of the small Iraqi town of Safwan in his reception room . . . he was a Baath Party apologist who was telling us how wonderful Saddam Hussein was, and he kept having flies crawling all over his mouth. Sitting with a dying camel, injured by a cluster bomb, in Kuwait. Making a headlong rush to the Caucasus in the middle of the night with a bunch of drunken Russians who weren't going to rest unless I saw the sun rise over the high Caucasus. These were the tiny moments in a life of adventures I've been immensely privileged to lead as a journalist," she says.

In short, journalism can take you to countries all over the world—places you never, ever expected to visit—and put you in contact with fascinating people you'd never have met otherwise, even while it gives you the opportunity to change the world for the better. We're humbled by the opportunities journalism has offered us.

If you don't have a sensation of apprehension
when you set out to find a story and a
swagger when you sit down to write it,
you are in the wrong business.

—A. M. ROSENTHAL, newspaper editor

The Right Personality for a Journalist

Interviews are at the heart of all good journalism. That means that journalists must feel comfortable speaking with strangers, no matter how personal or difficult the subject. If you're naturally shy, you'll have to learn to come out of your shell to be a successful reporter.

Journalists must also be hard workers. The work of journalism, particularly television reporting, looks a lot more glamorous than it really is. People who see Mike on the air doing a report on *60 Minutes* have missed the dozens if not hundreds of hours spent researching, setting up, and waiting for interviews to happen. The hours are long, especially during times of crisis, when journalists may work for days on end with almost no sleep. To be really successful in the supercompetitive world of journalism, reporters have to work harder than their competitors. Jill Abramson, managing editor of the *New York Times*, credits hard work and what journalists call "shoe leather"—working tirelessly to chase down leads—for her success as a reporter. She remembers one story she broke about illegal campaign contributions being made to President Bill Clinton's campaign. It started when she got hold of a list of all the contributors to the Democratic National Committee, the DNC. It was a public record, available to any reporter, but only Abramson seemed to spend the time to check it out. When Abramson started poring through the list, she noticed something interesting. "I lived in a pretty modest neighborhood in south Arlington, Virginia, not near where any Washington power brokers lived, and I noticed that one of the $50,000 donations to the DNC was from an address very close to my house in a truly terrible neighborhood. And so I drove over," Abramson recalls. "It was really this squalid little apartment building. It was absurd to think that anyone who lived there could have donated $50,000 to the DNC. And so for the next two weeks, my poor daughter, whenever she had a soccer game I would pick her up and then make her drive with me to all these little neighborhoods all over the Washington area—there were some in Maryland, too. And what I found over and over again were people living in very modest situations who were listed as a $100,000 donor or a $75,000 donor. My daughter was appalled to see me go up and knock on the doors of strangers. I had to explain to her that that's what journalism is all about."

Lin Garlick, executive editor of CBS Newspath—which provides footage and reports to about two hundred CBS-affiliated local stations around the country—also cites the benefits of burning some shoe leather. She recalls covering John McCain's run for president in 2000, when she worked alongside Phil Jones, one of CBS News' most experienced correspondents. "When I was covering McCain with Phil, I noticed some correspondents, some producers of note, would sometimes stay at their hotel and downlink the press conferences. But good old Jones and good old Lin, joint age well over a hundred, we'd be there," she says. She thinks that their diligence helped create high-quality reporting, because they had the background to hold the candidate accountable. "Phil Jones would stand there with this wry look on his face, tapping his notepad, and then he'd waggle his pen at McCain and say, 'But what you said last week . . . ,'" Garlick recalls. "You wouldn't have gotten that by staying at home, watching on a satellite feed."

Journalists also have to be brave, or at least bold. The profession often requires that reporters do things that are emotionally difficult, or expose themselves to some degree of danger. Reporters who cover war or conflict obviously put themselves in great peril. Such was the case when Mike flew to Tehran in December 1979 to interview the supreme leader of Iran, Ayatollah Ruhollah Khomeini. The ayatollah had just taken power after leading an Islamic revolution in that Middle Eastern nation, sending Iran's king, the shah, into exile. The Iran story touched America directly: on November 3, 1979, a group of radical students supporting Khomeini took fifty-two American diplomats hostage inside the U.S. Embassy, threatening their lives and keeping them in captivity for more than a year. The interview with Khomeini was a huge "get" for Mike, as it was considered a first look at the new face of Iran. But Khomeini did not naturally make for good television. The cleric was so conservative that he wouldn't even look at Mike during their interview. Khomeini stared at the floor or off into space as he talked.

So Mike asked him something that was sure to provoke him. After thinking long and hard about just how to phrase a question that would be certain to get a response but would not seem insulting, Mike quoted the words of the Egyptian president, Anwar Sadat—like Khomeini a Muslim, but someone who was a close friend of the deposed Iranian king. "Imam," Mike said, "President Sadat of Egypt says what you are doing is, quote, 'a disgrace to Islam.' And he calls you, Imam—forgive me, his words, not mine—'a lunatic.'" Mike covered his heart with his hand as he delivered the question, as if to request forgiveness for asking something so tough. The statement was so explosive that Khomeini's translator didn't dare relay it at first. "The translator was looking at me as though I was the lunatic for asking the question," Mike remembers. Before Khomeini answered, Mike had to confirm to the worried translator, "Yes, that's what I heard President Sadat say, on American television." The ayatollah did not speak English, but he sensed there was a problem. "Khomeini saw what was going on between me and the translator—and he was making up his mind exactly what he was going to do, if the question was finally translated for him. He started to answer and began to say,

'Sadat,'" Mike recalls. Khomeini was then speechless for several seconds as the question sank in. Finally, he said that Sadat could not be considered a Muslim because "he compromises with the enemies of Islam." The ayatollah's expression remained stony throughout, but Mike got to him.

Where did Mike get the chutzpah to ask this question?

"What are they gonna do? Make me a hostage?" Mike says, laughing. "You know something, I'm quite serious about that. That would be a hell of a news story, wouldn't it? 'Wallace has finally done himself in.'" Mike felt, as many journalists do, that there's some safety in being a reporter, and that Khomeini was unlikely to retaliate in response to a tough question. And while that was true for Mike, Khomeini was brutally harsh with others. "At that moment I didn't know yet that Khomeini was sending youngsters out to step on land mines, to permit his troops to advance in this war between Iran and Iraq."

Mike's interview with Khomeini was a major event, and the lunatic question would go down as one of the most provocative of Mike's long career. The legendary creator of *60 Minutes*, the late Don Hewitt, called the interview historic and "one of the great moments on television." Mike says that his boldness is probably one of the reasons he has succeeded as a journalist. "I haven't the slightest reluctance to break in and say, 'Hey, explain it' or 'Why?' or 'Because . . . ?' or 'Forgive me' or 'Come on!' They are wonderful interruptions. They suddenly make the object of your scrutiny explain," he says. And that's what a good journalist has to be willing to do—to keep pressing until he breaks new ground with his questions. (We'll talk in more detail about how to ask such questions later, in the interview chapter.)

Good journalists are often skeptics—but they need to be skeptical without being cynical. Linda Mason, the senior vice president of CBS News, remembers working on a story years ago about why the price of eggs was going up. It seemed like a simple matter of supply and demand to her, until she got a call from an anonymous source who claimed that an organization was limiting the egg supply. She almost ignored the source's claims but ended up following through on them to break a story. "Luckily, I listened to this other voice," Mason recalls. "It isn't always the easy solution that's the right answer. Sometimes the more complicated things are true."

Last, good journalists are humble. We've seen reporters lose their jobs for being prima donnas—treating their colleagues rudely or getting so full of themselves that they didn't do their work well. Most important, journalists must never let their egos get so big as to become insensitive to the plight of the people they cover.

The Right Education

Great reporters also need to have a broad understanding of the world. Journalists, after all, tend to be generalists, not specialists. You don't necessarily need to go to a good college or to college at all to be knowledgeable, although going to college certainly will help you compete against other would-be journalists who have their degrees. But you either need to be well educated or to educate yourself well. You need to know current events. You need to know civics, history, and geography. You should have read some of the great works of Western civilization and be up to date on current culture. The more you know about the world, the more likely you will be to use that knowledge to identify great stories. Plus, any news organization will give potential employees a test that includes questions about current news stories, recent history, and literature. And if you can't pass the test, you're simply not going to get hired.

More than that, you'll find that you need information about what's going on in the world on a daily basis. You can't fake being well rounded.

That said, it's not just what you know that's important—it's your ability to *learn*. Journalists are always being asked to become instant experts on the subjects they cover, and chances are, no matter how well rounded you are, you're going to need to study up on something quick. If you're going to write about a pop star's career, you'd better be able to quickly learn which of her singles were most successful, how she got her first big break, and whether she writes her own lyrics. If you're going to be writing about a city's new rent control legislation, you'll probably need to be able to give yourself a crash course on the housing market and landlord-tenant court. If you need to write about a financial fraudster, you'd better be able to learn enough about accounting practices to understand what he did wrong. One correspondent we know at CBS News once did 170 stories in one year on nearly 170 different topics. His ability to learn quickly has made him one of the network's top assets.

Students often ask whether it's better to study journalism or communication as an undergraduate, or to study something else, such as history, government, or a science. We think majoring in journalism is fine as long as it's part of a wide-ranging liberal arts education. Others disagree. "That's a terrible waste of a college degree," says Anderson. "Journalism is something you learn by doing. Writing is something you can be taught, and to take a writing course or two, I think, is great. But to major in something called journalism is much too vocational. It's like majoring in auto mechanics." Still, plenty of top journalists have majored in journalism—and many have not.

Whatever the benefits of a journalism degree, the fundamentals of journalism really only gel once students go out and start working. On-the-job experience is the best way to learn journalism. Get a good general education and then get yourself a job as an intern. Find opportunities to learn your trade, even if it means starting small. Neither of the authors had the opportunity to major in journalism, so most of our learning was done on the job. Internships are a great way to start. Mason, who oversees the CBS News internship program, makes a good point about the advantages of learning by doing: "When you start at the bottom, you get to make your mistakes at the bottom," she says.

These days, more than ever, journalism students need technical skills as well as critical thinking abilities if they are to stand out in this ultracompetitive business. "Start at the beginning. Learn how to handle a camera, learn how to handle a microphone, learn how to edit, and then do research," says Mike. The most marketable of Beth's students, whether they aspire to be print reporters or on-camera talent, know how to write for print, how to write for broadcast, how to use a camera, how to digitally edit television pieces, and how to design a website. The reason for this is that the Internet is creating convergence among media. On the Internet, all traditional forms of media—print, radio, photography, and broadcast—are morphing into one.

A look at the excellent *New York Times* website illustrates convergence perfectly. The site carries all the articles from the newspaper, but it's also filled with photo slide shows, blogs, podcasts, and even original video content. For example, its film reviewers now not only write film reviews but also write and appear in video segments that can be watched only on the newspaper's website. The websites of many other major news organizations—be they newspapers, magazines, radio, or television—have the same kind of multimedia approach. That means that the more ability a young journalist has to create all these kinds of reports, the more valuable he or she is likely to be to a news organization. "I'd be willing to do anything—floors, windows, toilets—whatever it takes to make you essential and flexible and in demand," jokes John M. Geddes, who serves along with Jill Abramson as a managing editor of the *New York Times*. "If writing comes naturally, learn editing basics. If you know how to design a printed page, learn how to create a website. If you know how to produce a Web page, learn how to do research for graphics. While specialists will be treasured, I believe generalists will be in demand during this business transition." A newspaper such as the *New York Times* has room for specialists because it has such a large staff, but the smaller your media outlet, the more valuable your technical skills are likely to be.

It is a newspaper's duty to
print the news and raise hell.

—WILBUR F. STOREY, newspaper owner

Information Versus Drama

Journalism, at its heart, exists to inform. That's pretty obvious. The very idea of "news" means it has to break new ground. But these days there's more emphasis than ever on sensationalism. Mike thinks sensationalism has gotten a bit of a bad name. "There is nothing wrong with the word *sensational*," he says. "Sensational is something that says, 'Hey, I didn't know that.'" But that said, journalists want their reports to be educational, not just titillating. How can one balance the need for hype that gets one's report noticed with the need to go out and get new information?

That's why this book is called *Heat and Light*. That's a phrase Mike often uses to describe what good journalism is all about. By *heat*, he means the emotional pull of a report—the kind of drama or conflict that gets people involved in a story. By *light*, he means information—the fresh knowledge that a well-reported story brings. "Light is the truth, heat is drama—what makes people tune in night after night after night," Mike explains. Heat and light together make for solid journalism. One without the other is less than ideal.

Mike came to his theory about heat and light in thinking about his signature interview style, the ambush. The ambush interview happens when a subject refuses all requests for an interview, and so a journalist tries to find the subject and interview him or her anyway, often just sticking a microphone into the subject's face and firing off questions. When doing an ambush, Mike, his producer, and their crew would stake the person out until he appeared. The person might be walking into his office, going to a restaurant, or attending an event, when Mike would pounce.

Ambush interviews were a sensation when Mike first started doing them, and he thinks they put the audience on his side. But then Mike began to sour on the idea, because the drama such interviews created wasn't enough to make ambushes worthwhile. "When you begin to do it in such a way that it becomes apparent that what you are after is drama, heat rather than light, then enough already. We are not getting light, and the heat is contrived," he says.

That's why Mike eventually stopped doing ambush interviews in all but rare circumstances. When Mike did do them, he would talk the idea over with *60 Minutes* creator and executive producer Don Hewitt first to make sure the ends justified the means. "Hewitt and I asked ourselves, what are we after? Are we after light or heat? The heat business can be fascinating," Mike explains. "There is a certain drama there, but that wears out pretty quickly."

What's an example of it wearing thin? Although we both respect him, we think that the early work of Geraldo Rivera sometimes erred too much toward heat and too little toward light. Rivera didn't start doing ambush interviews until after Mike started doing them, and Mike thinks Rivera started doing them too often, and emphasizing heat over light. "To see him running down the street to get the interview diminishes the credibility of the reporter who is doing the interview. Nothing is worth that. Nothing," says Mike. These kinds of interviews are fair as long as you tried to get a sit-down interview first and really need to speak with the person being ambushed, but they should always be treated as a last resort.

Although the ideas of heat and light came to Mike with regard to ambush interviews, the concept carries through to reporting in general. Every good correspondent should seek to shed light with his or her reporting. Heat is great as an accompaniment to light, because drama or conflict helps make the light of an article shine deeper and brighter. Heat and light together make for reports that people are likely to watch closely or read through to the end, maximizing the amount of new information that they absorb. Heat and light together also help attract viewers or readers. We hope that the advice in this book will help create journalists who can create both heat and light—and whose work will be both passionate and compassionate as it sheds light on important issues.

The role of the journalist is indispensable, and as reviled as reporters may intermittently be, they are still highly respected when they pursue the truth and obtain positive results.

—HELEN THOMAS, journalist and author

What Is Objectivity?

When the authors were coming along in our careers, we were taught that journalists should be objective. That meant that journalists should put their personal feelings on hold and create reports with balance and without bias, based only on the facts. Of course, that's hard to do, because all people have feelings and opinions. Yet most seasoned journalists usually manage, with practice, to suspend those feelings, or at least shunt them into the background, when doing their work. Mike, citing the example of three of America's most influential anchormen, says that's a key to success. "Peter Jennings used to keep the news at arm's length. In other words, he was not part of the news. His views of the news were not part of the story. The same thing was true with Tom Brokaw. They both kept the news at arm's length. I have had nothing but respect and adoration for Dan Rather, but he got caught up in the news. His reaction became part of the news. And that's one of the things that brought him low." We're not fans of the kind of opinionated chat that some anchors do before or after a story, where they will declare something "cute" or "sad." We just don't think anchors or reporters should give their opinions at all. To give analysis of events based on their experience, yes. To give us their personal opinions of things, no.

Objectivity is the very basis of print reporting as well. "When you pick up 'All the News That's Fit to Print,' you have the sense that these people who are putting out the *New York Times* care deeply about it, take it seriously, and separate the news from the commentary," explains Mike. "Damn seldom does opinion find its way into the news column. There is an op-ed page," he explains, referring to the page across from the editorial page in most newspapers, where opinion articles appear (*op-ed* in fact means "opposite the editorials"). And yet the American public repeatedly gives the press very low ratings for objectivity—particularly newspapers, which we find disappointing given that most news organizations, particularly newspapers, are actually trying hard every day to maintain their objectivity.

Objective journalism was epitomized by the late, great Walter Cronkite, the anchorman for CBS News from the 1950s until 1981. Cronkite was one of the most important journalists of his generation, shaping America's understanding of such events as the war in Vietnam, the race to the moon, and the Watergate scandal. Cronkite consistently showed up in polls as one of the most trusted men in America. The reason? He told the news straight. He gave the facts and tried to keep his personal opinions out of it. "Why was Cronkite called the most trusted man in America?" asks Mike. "Because he was a serious reporter. He respected his audience." The foundation of Cronkite's success was his relentless commitment to objectivity and balance. He tried to give his viewers the raw material they needed to make their own decisions about the world's most pressing issues. He told them what to think *about*, not what to think.

Yet the question of whether journalists should be neutral or should advocate goes back almost to the beginning of television news. Arguably the greatest American journalist of the modern age was Edward R. Murrow, who reported for CBS News from 1938 to 1961. Murrow was not trained as a journalist. His education was in drama. But he was a natural storyteller, a fantastic writer, and an awe-inspring broadcaster, with a voice that rumbled with importance. Every journalism student should listen to some of Murrow's rooftop broadcasts from London, when he covered World War II for CBS News. Not only did Murrow write with blazing originality, but his delivery on both radio and television was hypnotic. "He was special. I don't think there's ever been anyone like him," says Kalb, who was recruited to join CBS News by Murrow, and overlapped with him there for a short time.

Murrow was also a man with a moral compass, with strong feelings about the world and a sense of outrage when events or people didn't measure up to his expectations. In his news reports, Murrow didn't just explain what was going on—he often added what he thought about it. His reporting would probably be labeled "advocacy journalism" today, but Murrow thought the role of a journalist was not just to report what was happening but to add his own expert analysis. "I have reason to know, as do many of you, that when the evidence on a controversial subject is fairly and calmly presented, the public recognizes it for what it is—an effort to illuminate rather than to agitate," Murrow said back in 1958.

Even though he was the most important journalist of his time, Murrow's refusal to keep his opinions out of his reporting eventually led to his demise. The head of CBS, broadcasting pioneer William S. Paley, hated controversy, or at least he hated the financial consequences of controversy. Although he and Murrow were close friends for years, they had a falling-out over Murrow's opinionated reports. Paley, being the owner of the network, won the fight, and Murrow ending up being shunted to the side of CBS News and eventually left television. "I think that the business was beginning to change, and Murrow didn't change," explains Kalb. "It was the very beginning of the idea of pictures making big, big bucks, of millions and hundreds of millions of dollars being made by a network. And I imagine Paley didn't want anything to upset that." Murrow would not and could not accept limits on his capacity to tell the news.

So future generations at CBS News, starting with Walter Cronkite, followed the objective style of journalism that Paley preferred. And that included Mike. "At CBS, if you let your own opinions find their way into your coverage, you did it at your own peril," Mike remembered. "I had editors who would say to me, 'Hey, Mike, we are objective,' when from time to time my own personal opinion began to creep in to my coverage. I would be called on the carpet. 'Mike, you are talking for CBS News.' And that meant that we were answerable to the people that Bill Paley had hired to make sure that we remained objective." Objectivity remains paramount at CBS News to this day. "Most journalists have lived a long time and we all have opinions, but as a journalist we are supposed to be able to rise above these opinions and to be able to sort through a story as it lays itself out—that we don't bring into bearing our feelings one way or another," explains Linda Mason. "If the audience thinks that a CBS person feels on one side [of an issue], they're going to think that CBS somehow isn't fair."

Objectivity can be awfully hard to maintain, especially when the topic evokes serious emotion. Early in his career, Russ Mitchell, the CBS News anchor, was sent to cover a Ku Klux Klan event, even though the group is openly hostile to blacks and Mitchell is African American. "They sent the only reporter they had that day, which would have been me, to a Klan rally, which was interesting," Mitchell says with a laugh. "I clearly have issues with the Klan." Yet he remembers going out of his way to write an objective and balanced story about what happened, quoting both supporters and opponents of the group. "Once you're putting it on TV, once you're writing it down, you have an obligation to be objective," he explains. It can also be nearly impossible to maintain objectivity during crises and catastrophes. After the 2010 Haitian earthquake, for example, many journalists openly empathized with those affected and voiced frustration over the slow pace of rescue efforts.

The Internet age has added a new dimension to the objectivity game—journalists now need to watch what they say not just in their reports but on their personal blogs and sites and on social networking sites such as Facebook and MySpace. "In the last election some of our younger people were writing on Facebook that they were thrilled to be working in a newsroom where Obama was getting so much attention, or they felt strongly about McCain, and you can't do that," says Mason. "Anybody who works for CBS News, you shouldn't be able to tell who they are in favor of because they should tell the same story for both candidates." CBS News now reminds staff to be extremely careful about what they write on social networking sites, and to apply the network's existing ethical standards to their posts on Facebook, MySpace, Twitter, and other such sites.

Some news organizations now have written policies to limit what their correspondents say on social networking sites. The *New York Times* issued such guidelines in 2009, saying that although the sites are "remarkably useful reporting tools," they require care. "Personal blogs and 'tweets' represent you to the outside world just as much as an 800-word article does," says the *Times* code of conduct. "If you have or are getting a Facebook page, leave blank the section that asks about your political views, in accordance with the Ethical Journalism admonition to do nothing that might cast doubt on your or *The Times*' political impartiality in reporting the news." The Associated Press' guidelines are similar and are aimed at "upholding the AP's reputation for fairness and impartiality, which has been one of our chief assets for more than 160 years. These guidelines do not break new ground—they are consistent with the rest of our Statement of News Values and Principles. They just take into account the new realities of the social-networking world." The technology may have changed, but the essentials of objectivity remain the same.

I think perfect objectivity is an unrealistic goal;
fairness, however, is not.

—MICHAEL POLLAN, journalist, author, and professor

Do We Need Objectivity Anymore?

Plenty of American journalists have abandoned objectivity in the years since Murrow. In the 1960s and '70s, reporters such as Hunter S. Thompson in print and David Brinkley on television made it perfectly clear how they felt. And today, plenty of journalists produce great stories that blend analysis with opinion. Take a look at *Rolling Stone* or the *New Yorker* and you'll see that opinionated reporting can be a wonderful thing. The reality is that both objective and advocacy reporting can be good. We need to trust news consumers to choose the kind of reporting they like best.

Nevertheless, we're at risk of being dragged into a world

where opinion dominates objectivity, thanks both to the influence of the Internet and to changes in the TV news business. Even if people have no new facts to add to an Internet discussion, they almost always have an opinion to share. And in television, a few networks have found that dealing in opinion is easier, cheaper, and more profitable than old-fashioned objectivity. These include Fox News Channel, the first news network to bring a political agenda to the forefront, and MSNBC, which searched for an identity for many years before finding one based in opinion shows. The success of those networks is now making lots of people rethink the need for objective reporting.

We're shocked and dismayed at times when we see how far some TV channels have moved from objectivity. We see anchors who are enchanted by the sound of their own voice and spend too much time giving out their opinions instead of reporting the news. One of the worst offenders is Lou Dobbs, formerly of CNN. Although Dobbs has had a long and storied career and hosted a highly successful nightly business program, Mike says it seems like Dobbs is running for president instead of presenting the news. "I think to myself Lou, you sound like such a damn fool," Mike says.

The problem with Dobbs' recent work is that the anchorman takes himself too seriously, puts too much of his own opinion into his work, and has become too much of a populist. What annoyed us most about Dobbs' CNN show was seeing him read fan mail on the air, as if to emphasize that he and his viewers all feel the same way about the world. "To watch him is to know that it's a cult. And he is the cult leader," says Mike. Dobbs himself admits that his show, *Lou Dobbs Tonight*, did not follow the classic rules of journalism. "It's very different from any program you'll see on TV, by intention," Dobbs told the *New Yorker*. "What you won't see on our broadcast is 'fair and balanced journalism.' You will not see 'objective journalism.' The truth is not 'fair and balanced.'" Despite these criticisms, Dobbs' success is undeniable; his CNN show grabbed a large and loyal audience, and in fact many of his viewers tuned in to CNN precisely to hear what he had to say about things.

Hosts such as Dobbs stay on the air, as do the opinion-based cable news networks including Fox News Channel and MSNBC, because some Americans have a real appetite for opinion shows. But those programs aren't popular with everyone. "Opinions are cheap and easy. Reporting is expensive and hard," says Neil Hickey, a veteran reporter who now teaches at the Columbia Graduate School of Journalism. "The cable news channels in prime time have nothing but opinion, and usually opinion traffickers shouting at the top of their lungs. I'd rather they simply tell me what happened, and I can make up my own mind."

Fox News Channel is particularly interesting to us, because it pioneered a new way of approaching television news. Fox News calls itself an objective news channel—in fact, its main slogans are "Fair and Balanced" and "We Report, You Decide." But analyses of Fox News Channel by scholars and media groups show a clear slant toward conservative, Republican views, not the bipartisan approach you would expect if it were truly fair and balanced. Likewise, the network's biggest star, Bill O'Reilly, claims that his show is a spin-free zone, but that's really not true. "I think that he misrepresents himself, in the same way that critics say Fox News misrepresents itself, because the spin does not stop with him," Beth says. "In fact, that spin intensifies with him. Maybe other people's spin ends there, but his spin begins." O'Reilly's typical behavior illustrates exactly the difference between heat and light in journalism. "If you yell at your guests because you don't like what they are saying, tell them to shut up, and cut off their microphone, then we go from light to heat. We have left the field of journalism," Beth maintains. "There's no doubt about that, but it's made him millions," Mike responds. In fact, O'Reilly is so prominent that when Mike profiled him for *60 Minutes,* the piece was chosen to kick off the 2004–05 season.

Fox News Channel regularly has the highest ratings of all cable news stations during prime time—beating even CNN, the network that invented cable news. It's done so by putting opinion front and center, although Fox, like MSNBC, also has plenty of straight news. Fox has also assembled a stellar team, including Mike's son Chris Wallace, who has worked at Fox News Channel since 2003 after a distinguished career reporting for NBC and ABC. His take is that Fox is able to do both objective-style news and opinion-based shows—and that viewers know the difference. He says that nobody would characterize Fox News' prime-time hours, with hosts such as Bill O'Reilly, Sean Hannity, and Glenn Beck, as news. "They're not; they're commentary. And I think that's fine. You know, a newspaper has an op-ed page, and that's what people want in prime time," says Wallace. "But I think if you look at the vast majority of Fox News during the broadcast day particularly, not at night, it is straight news." Wallace says Fox plays things straight in its hard news and on his show, *Fox News Sunday.* The Fox formula has brought the channel huge profits and a loyal audience. And a 2010 poll finds that Fox News Channel is the nation's most trusted television network for news.

We don't mind there being opinion-driven television on the air—let the free market determine whether those kinds of channels really have an audience. However, we'd prefer calling a spade a spade. If Fox marketed itself as "America's conservative television news network," and if MSNBC openly called itself "America's liberal television news network," we'd probably like that much more than the way they present themselves now. In fact, liberal groups have been so incensed by Fox's use of the slogan "Fair and Balanced" that they have appealed to the Federal Trade Commission and the U.S. Patent and Trademark Office to try to force Fox to stop using it, without success.

People coming up in the business now need to understand the success of Fox News Channel because it's had a huge effect not only on cable news but on the whole broadcast business. There are more high-octane show anchors than ever—and also more correspondents and anchors who chat in a casual way on the air, like old friends, as on Fox News. All over television news programs, there are also more flashy bottom-of-the-screen crawls than ever before, and graphics featuring the American flag are everywhere. All that can be traced to the success of Fox News.

These networks are here to stay, and the prevalence of opinion in cable news presents a problem for young journalists. "It's obviously hard to say to my students who watch Fox that they need to be objective," explains Beth. "They say, 'What do you mean we should be objective? Look at Bill O'Reilly. Turn on Fox News. They're not objective, so we don't need to be objective anymore.' "

The bottom line is that when you're Bill O'Reilly, you can be subjective. But if you're just beginning, unless you're working for an opinion-based news show, you should stick with the traditional model of staying objective in your reporting. For the majority of news outlets, this is still your best way to stay credible. We haven't yet moved to a model of journalism where people who are just starting out can be subjective all the time.

And remember, even the stars of subjective reporting mastered the craft of objective reporting first. O'Reilly, for instance, spent years perfecting his craft as an anchor and correspondent for various local and national newscasts before he became the pundit we know from Fox News. Hunter S. Thompson spent almost a decade laboring in the trenches of newspaper writing before he penned *Hell's Angels.* It's a bit like art—even Pablo Picasso spent years mastering classical painting styles, developing the skills that would allow him to experiment with more avant-garde techniques such as cubism. In journalism as in art, you can't move ahead until you've mastered the basics.

Make an earnest and conscientious journal;
establish its reputation for truth and reliability,
frankness and independence.

—JOSEPH MEDILL, newspaper owner, Chicago mayor

Fairness and Balance

Another of the things journalists must do well is to be fair—fair to the people they interview, and fair to the subjects they cover. In general, something is fair if it is free from bias, honest, and impartial. And most journalists have their own way of making sure they've been fair. To Linda Mason, who's in charge of news standards at CBS News, fairness is "if you go out of your way to tell both sides of the story." Ron Blum, a sportswriter for the Associated Press wire service, says fairness means being evenhanded—and it's one of his top concerns. "Are you being fair to all perspectives of the story? If you are mentioned in a negative light in a story, have you been given a chance to have your say?" he asks. "I'd like to think that I treat all the people I cover fairly. Bud Selig, the baseball commissioner, may yell and scream at me on occasion and be critical of things I have written, but I think that later, after emotions have subsided, he'd say I was fair." To Scott Pelley, the *60 Minutes* correspondent, fairness equals honesty. "You can tell when you've been honest, and when you haven't been honest, and that really is what we're talking about here," he says. "And it's just so important, I think, for a journalist to be like a scientist, and not care what the answer is—just care whether you have the right answer. And that's when you know you're being honest and fair with people." Fairness is related to objectivity, but it has to do with the final product rather than the process. Even if you don't succeed in putting all your personal feelings aside and being totally objective, you can still create a report that is fair.

Fairness requires diligent reporting, and reporting all sides of a story. "I don't even start to sit down and write until I've stamped out all the nagging embers of uncertainty as far as I can," says Kim Murphy. "This involves, in issues that are in dispute, calling people on all possible sides of an issue to see what they say. It is always amazing to get an account of something that happened from one guy, then call up somebody else and hear him describe it in a completely different way." Reporters usually try to be fair, but they can miss the mark if they're not accurate or balanced. "I remember when I lived in Russia and was writing a story about a political party," remembers Beth, "and I went to a friend for analysis who was involved in politics and hated this party. Looking back, I realized that I inadvertently picked up his slant on things and put that into my article." Journalists can easily fall into this kind of trap when they don't know their subject matter very well.

One of the most important aspects of fairness is quoting people accurately. Fairness requires that you never twist people's words to make it sound like they meant something other than what they said. People's quotations can be misconstrued if you take them out of context—linking up an answer not to the question that elicited it but to another question, or editing an answer to change the meaning. Shows such as *60 Minutes* have the resources to have someone on staff to do nothing but double-check that interview quotes have been used accurately and fairly. "We have one person whose job it is to read every interview and to look at what you have taken out of it, and to make sure that what you have taken out of it is representative of what the interviewee meant and said and in the proper context," explains Robert Anderson. "That's there as a backup and it's good to have, but one very rarely needs that backup because we know what we are doing, and we want to be fair." But few news organizations can afford to do this, meaning that journalists have to police themselves and make fairness a conscious priority.

That said, even the best journalists can be accused of being unfair. Mike was sued by the general who ran the U.S. effort in Vietnam, General William Westmoreland, over allegations of unfair tactics. A 1982 CBS News documentary called *The Uncounted Enemy* alleged that Westmoreland and his staff intentionally underreported the number of North Vietnamese fighters by about half to help keep the United States in the war. After Westmoreland complained, CBS News undertook an internal investigation, which found that Mike and his team had in fact broken some network news-gathering standards. For instance, parts of different questions were patched together unfairly, and the interview was shot in a way that made the general seem nervous and untrustworthy. Westmoreland sued for $120 million, and although he ended up dropping the case during the trial, Mike's reputation took a battering over the incident. It goes to show that although the best reporters try to be fair and have editors to check their work, there can still be times where reports come out with a slant.

The reporter's best resource in the quest for fairness is to have a good editor or producer looking over his or her shoulder. Editors do a lot more than tweak words. They help keep journalists out of trouble. They make sure that ethical and legal standards are being met. They make sure that stories have the proper background and have been put in context. They help brainstorm about ideas, issues, and people to interview.

"We all need editors," says Mike. "If you take news seriously, you need an editor." Mike credits much of his success at *60 Minutes* to the steady hand of the show's founder and chief producer, the late Don Hewitt, who had a magical touch when it came to putting together diverse elements into a harmonious whole. But that doesn't mean they always agreed on everything. "Hewitt and I would argue with blood on the floor, and I mean seriously. And he would storm out of the editing room or storm out of the studio when we were taking a look at the piece—really volatile," he recalls. "It was one of the joys of working there, because you were working together on a story. It wasn't about who was in charge." And it wasn't personal. Mike says he and Hewitt never held a grudge against each other after one of their fights. It was all about the final product.

Chris Wallace says that a good editor or producer ends up making correspondents look smarter. "I often say on a story there are a thousand decisions that have to be made—who you're going to book, what are you going to ask them in the interview, how are you going to assemble the material, how are you going to edit it down, what pictures are you going to put in," he explains. "And usually by the time your editor—or in this case, your executive producer—sees your story, nine hundred and fifty of those decisions have been made. I think it's awfully important to have a fresh set of eyes who isn't as involved, who doesn't have all the background you do, to come help you make the last fifty. To say, 'Gee, that isn't clear' or 'That isn't fair' or 'I'm not sure I understand it' or 'I think that's really off the point and redundant' or 'Gee, we've got to cut this down and this is the part that I think we should cut down.'"

Be warned that maintaining fairness and accuracy takes hard work and vigilance, from both editors and their reporters.

2

THE QUESTION: THE ART OF STORY GENERATION AND RESEARCH

Bad news goes about in clogs,
good news in stockinged feet.

—WELSH PROVERB

James Ford is a familiar face to many early risers in New York City. As the lead reporter for the *WPIX Morning News*, he's live on Channel 11 covering the main story each day. Ford goes live approximately once every thirty minutes during the four and a half hours his program's on the air. That's a very long show by broadcasting standards, but Ford and his colleagues fill it every morning, and do so with a skeleton staff—as do hundreds of other local news broadcasts all over the country. He says that his team is particularly lucky, in that there's always something interesting to cover in New York City. "We ask ourselves, 'What's the story of the day?'—the thing that's most relevant and interesting to our audience—and make the decision that way," Ford says. "That doesn't always mean breaking news. Sometimes politics, transportation, weather, and maybe even sports once in a blue moon ends up leading our broadcast." The ability to pick unique and interesting stories can make or break you.

This chapter will focus on those "before" parts of doing a story—story identification, story generation, research, and preparation. These are key skills. If your "before" skills are weak, it's hard to get to the "during" part of journalism. Good preparation helps create sound journalism. What you create at the end depends on the raw materials you're able to gather—and the better your process of preparing the story, the better raw material you are likely to have.

Deciding What's Newsworthy

A story is more than something that happens. It's something important, something significant, or something novel. Experienced reporters tend to have a highly developed ability to spot a story. "My gut tells me what it is, and that gut is a result of years of experience," says Lin Garlick, executive editor of CBS Newspath. Even if you don't have years of experience, you can learn what's worth a story.

Award-winning *60 Minutes* correspondent Scott Pelley has one of the most specific set of criteria we've seen for choosing topics. "I have a five-level filter that I put all stories through at first blush to see if they're worthy of consideration," Pelley explains. "Is it important—is it the kind of thing that would lead the broadcast? Is it the kind of thing that has real meaning for our audience—is it a big deal? Are we exposing an injustice—are blood, sweat, or tears involved? Is it an epic story of human struggle? And is it the kind of story that brings honor and stature to the broadcast? One does not have to satisfy all five, but if you've got three out of five, it's going to be a great story." If you watch Pelley's reports—and we highly recommend you take a look at some of his work if you're not familiar with it—you can easily see how they reflect his checklist.

And Pelley says that any enterprising young journalist can use those same five filters. "All five were in a story that I did at one big hospital in Las Vegas, which was closing its outpatient oncology clinic for indigent patients because the economic crisis had blown a hole in the state budget and they had to start cutting things off that were vital. So you had indigent cancer patients being told, 'Sorry, you have nowhere to go now. You can move out of the state, you can die, but those are pretty much your options at this point.' You don't have to go to Darfur to find that story. In fact, it's a more compelling story when you find that story right here at home among the people who are feeling the pain of the economic downturn, for example. So these stories do not have to be exotic, and in fact they're probably better when they're not." Stories are relative to an audience. What is a story to a radio station in Boise may not qualify as news to a monthly magazine in Miami. But the essential elements of novelty and importance always have to be there.

There are two kinds of stories: what journalists call *hard news* and *soft news*. Hard news means things that have just happened and are noteworthy, including important events all over the world, new government programs, or breakthroughs in medicine. Soft news means stories without a specific time element, often focusing on trends. Soft news stories are also known as *features*. Hard news relates to today's events. Soft news can often sit around for a day, a week, or a month and not lose its intrinsic value. When Iranian officials try to fake an election, that's hard news. When Iranian women start having more nose jobs because that part of their face is most prominent when wearing a head covering, as the government requires, that's soft news.

Often, news executives look for something known as a *news peg* as a way to make soft news stories appear timely. A news peg is a hard news event that's related to the topic of a soft news story; presenting the hard news makes the related soft news seem more important. Let's say that ABC had prepared a soft news story about how more and more men are having plastic surgery. Such a story could run on any day. But if the American Medical Association releases a report saying that plastic surgery for men is the fastest-growing area of elective procedures, then producers at ABC might say, "Hey, here's a news peg on which we can hang that story."

Whether the story is hard or soft, editors and reporters consider six factors when deciding what stories deserve mention. Many of these depend on the type of media, the location, and the audience:

PROXIMITY. How close are the events to your audience? Journalists often cover news because it is happening nearby. A local paper may cover the governor because she is in town, or may cover a rock band because it's appearing nearby. Proximity is important, particularly to local news media, but isn't paramount. Some media, such as websites, don't really have to consider proximity, because their audience is scattered across the country, or perhaps around the world. And newspapers, even local ones, routinely write about news that's going on halfway around the world.

IMPACT. Events that have an impact on a news outlet's audience are usually worth reporting. The more direct the impact on the audience, the more likely it is that a piece of news will make it onto the air or into print. For instance, the average viewer of a network evening news broadcast is about sixty-five years old, so the producers often choose stories that are likely to be of interest to older viewers. These broadcasts tend to run heavy on coverage of medical breakthroughs and entitlement programs for the elderly such as Medicare and Social Security.

Measuring a story's direct impact is easy; trickier is figuring out which stories have enough indirect impact to be worth covering. For instance, even though events going on in China, Brazil, or Russia may not directly affect people in the United States, that doesn't mean international affairs don't merit coverage.

And there are exceptions to the impact filter as well—sometimes news that doesn't really have an impact is interesting enough for its own sake to be worth covering. Beth remembers working on a story about commercials being filmed up on the Russian Mir space station. "I don't think any of our viewers would ever get up to Mir, or actually have a commercial filmed there," she remembers. "It was just a fun story, with some nice pictures. Years later, I can still remember how in one of the commercials we showed, the cosmonauts would float bubbles of milk around in the weightlessness of space and then catch them on their tongues. It made me smile, so I assumed it would make our viewers smile, too."

TIMELINESS. Hard news always has to be timely. The very definition of *news* is that it's something that has just happened. Rarely, one may get some news that happened a week, month, or year ago, but such news always is accompanied by an explanation as to why journalists are reporting it only now—as when old documents are unearthed by current-day researchers.

Modern technology has led to drastic changes in what qualifies as timely. As late as the 1960s, television reports were shot on film, which took days to transport from the place where it was shot to a place where it could be broadcast. For that era, two or three days was timely. But today, more than ever, people want their news immediately. And technological advances mean they can get it immediately, from almost anywhere in the world. Reporters now routinely use computers and satellite telephones to send text or video from almost anywhere on the planet.

CONFLICT. A report doesn't necessarily have to have a conflict, but the most compelling news stories often do. The conflict may be between people, such as two competing politicians. It may be between nations, such as Israel and Lebanon. Or it may be between competing ideas, such as whether or not to allow gay marriage. Conflict creates drama—heat—and that helps grab the audience's attention.

PROMINENCE. The prominence of the people involved in the news often determines its importance. If a regular citizen is mugged walking down Michigan Avenue, the crime is unlikely to make it into the Chicago papers. But if the mayor gets mugged, it will likely be the lead story in the papers and in broadcast.

BUZZ. *Buzz* refers to what people tend to be talking about at their job or around the dinner table. In general, if people are talking about someone or something, then they're likely to want to hear even more about that person or thing. On *60 Minutes*, for example, attempts are often made to land an interview with whomever Americans are discussing, whether it's a celebrity or someone who has done something important. Buzz is a little different from the other criteria for judging newsworthiness, because buzz is usually set off by something already in the news. It's a resonance in the story that keeps people interested.

Often buzz has to do with celebrity news. There are times when so many people are talking about some celebrity's story that it may actually become legitimate news for "serious" news outlets. Consider the coverage of Michael Jackson's death and you'll see what we mean. Every news outlet covered it—even über-serious outlets such as the *Wall Street Journal* and the *Nation*. "Sometimes it's not bad to talk about Brad and Angelina having twins. It's not bad to talk about Tom and Katie having a baby. You know, let's get off our high horses here," says Garlick. Some news outlets thrive on following that kind of news, while others wrestle with it—both because they think that celebrities deserve some privacy and because they want to follow more serious news. Take the first day of school for first daughters Sasha and Malia Obama. The public's interest in the story was high. Not only was the new first family attracting attention for breaking racial barriers, but it had been many years since young children had lived in the White House, making the Obama girls' first day at school a double-header in terms of interest. NBC, like most major news organizations, covered the story, but with a caveat: we'll give you what you want now, but then we're going to leave these girls alone. "Those of us who are parents can commiserate," said anchor Brian Williams. "Switching schools in the middle of the year is tough enough, so we'll cover their dad, the president-elect, and their mom when she makes news, and in the meantime, we will try to let Sasha and Malia do their job, making new friends at their new school."

There's always been celebrity news around, but it seems to us that there's more of it now than ever before—because viewers want it. "You've got a few senior producers here, we all like to yap about things, and if something catches our imagination—we're a pretty diverse group—we think, 'Well, maybe that captures the world's or the viewers' imagination,'" says Garlick. "And we say, 'Hey, let's do it. What the heck.'" She remembers that when Tom Cruise and Katie Holmes had their baby, she sent a correspondent out to their mansion to file reports and do live shots for the CBS local news affiliates. "And we had so many stations fighting over the live shots," she remembers. News executives try to give the people what they want, and for the most part, that seems to be whatever is causing buzz. As Mike puts it, "We're trying to get a lot of people to tune in. How do you get a lot of people to tune in? You give them sensational stuff." That flexibility has been one source of the success of *60 Minutes*.

Journalism never admits that nothing much is happening.

—MASON COOLEY, professor

Finding a Story

Generating ideas for stories is a key skill for journalists. There's no one way to come up with an idea. "Where a story comes from I liken to lightning striking, and I have absolutely no idea where the lightning is going to strike next," says Robert Anderson, Mike's producer. "I have depended on the kindness of strangers, and on my associate producers and on my correspondents to really help in that regard. The obvious way is skimming a lot of papers and reading a lot of magazines."

READ EVERYTHING. One way to find good stories is to read. If you're working for a national news outlet, search through local press from various cities to find interesting stories that have not yet reached a national audience. Read small newspapers, magazines, journals, broadcast news sites, and blogs. It's also important to look through primary sources for possible stories, including government and privately funded studies, research reports, the websites of nongovernmental organizations, and press releases. The list of places to look is almost endless. Internet access to publications all around the world means it's easier than ever before to read what is going on in other places and to pick up stories from far away. Before the Internet, the only way to read, say, the *Des Moines Register* would be either to buy it in Iowa or at a specialty newsstand or to get it by mail. Now, that paper and thousands of others are instantly available 24/7. If you're working for a local news outlet, read the other media covering your town—not to steal stories, but to identify areas you may not be covering well enough. Look at news coverage in comparable towns and cities, too—you might find angles and approaches worth exploring in your area. When you're covering local news, it's especially important to scan primary sources such as websites, reports, and flyers for possible stories.

Story ideas can also come from news agencies such as the Associated Press, Reuters, Bloomberg News, or Agence France-Presse. Most news organizations subscribe to at least one news agency, and some subscribe to several. These kinds of agencies specialize in delivering breaking news, but over the past few years, they have all put more emphasis on features, analysis, and investigative stories. Blogs and social networking sites didn't exist until recently, but they also can provide leads on stories. During the 2010 Haitian earthquake, for example, journalists were able to find survivors and families looking for loved ones via the Internet.

SOURCES. Although there's plenty of written material out there to draw from, many of the best stories come from sources. People often call or write in with story ideas. And journalists build relationships with people as they work, relationships that often lead to stories. This is why news organizations are often organized on a system of *beats*. A beat is an area the reporter covers for months or years at a time, such as politics, crime, or health care. Having a beat not only allows reporters to gain expertise in an area but also gives them a way to form relationships with people involved in their beat. A city hall reporter, for example, might forge sources among a mayor's staff, city council members, or civil servants at municipal agencies.

Many of the top reporters get their best stories by cultivating sources, building relationships over weeks and months. "One of my biggest scoops I got just because I was out walking around the White House and saw somebody," says Chris Wallace. It was one of his sources—someone with whom he had built a relationship. "Somebody will tell you something that they probably shouldn't tell you because they kind of trust you, they like you, and they want to show off that they know something that you don't," he explains. And when you're looking for something that your competitors don't have, your contacts can make the difference. Ron Blum, who covers sports for the Associated Press, also uses his sources to fact-check information. "Contacts help get you information that might not otherwise be public, and longtime contacts that you can trust help you discern what's true and what's false, especially important in an era when the rise of blogs of various accuracy has caused more disinformation to be out in public," he says. "Contacts often help you knock down stories as false."

The relationship between a reporter and a source usually takes time to develop. The source may tell something to the reporter and ask that it be reported, or that it *not* be reported, then wait and see what the reporter does with that information before providing more. Sources usually want evidence that reporters can keep their word before turning over more-sensitive information. "Always, every day, you're out gathering information, writing stories, and hoping the credibility you gain by writing accurate, well-balanced articles will give your sources the confidence to talk to you again the next time you come to the trough, or better yet, call you up or email you when they hear something interesting," explains Kim Murphy of the *Los Angeles Times*. "I drank away a good part of my life in the local bar near the county Hall of Administration, swilling with aides to the Board of Supervisors. I would retire to the restroom periodically during the night and scratch down information they had told me ill-advisedly during the evening. The next day, I'd call them up and badger them into helping me get it on the record. They took my calls because they *knew* me, knew that I was basically a good guy." The classic example of building sources? Deep Throat, the long-anonymous official who helped reporters Bob Woodward and Carl Bernstein of the *Washington Post* get the Watergate story.

Of course, sources can be useful even if you don't always cover the same topic. "I've never had a beat per se, so cultivating longtime sources to quote repeatedly in pieces is not something that's been part of my experience," says Michael Bronner, an investigative reporter who was a producer for CBS News before becoming a contributor to the magazine *Vanity Fair*. "Writing long, narrative stories—and writing on a diversity of subjects, as you often do at a magazine—you often end up needing sources highly specific to the story at hand, so you end up (usually in a mad flurry) searching for, finding, cultivating and ultimately coming to know a new roster of sources for each story." Those people not only make sure you've explained everything correctly, they also make sure you got the context correct. "My most important long-term sources are people with deep experience in a particular area that I can go back to for perspective or a reality check. One, for example, is a forty-year Defense Intelligence Agency veteran—a guy with vast experience and a deeply analytical mind who often helps me understand what the information and experience I've gained for a particular story means in the broader historical context," Bronner explains. You may not even quote a source like that in a piece, but it adds value by making your reporting deeper, more accurate, and more nuanced.

Sometimes ideas come from other journalists. That's how Mike came across euthanasia advocate Jack Kevorkian. "A reporter from the *Detroit Free Press* told us," Mike recalls. "He said, 'You have to talk to Kevorkian because of who he is, and I'll talk to you about how to get hold of the tape of him performing euthanasia on Tom Young with the acceptance of the mother and brother and family. They want the public to see it.'" That turned into a highly watched and highly controversial report.

As you build your journalistic experience, you get more skilled at picking topics and subjects. For instance, a few years ago Mike wanted to do a piece on former Massachusetts governor and Republican presidential hopeful Mitt Romney—but the chief producer of *60 Minutes*, Jeff Fager, wasn't really interested in Romney at first. Mike knew from all his years of doing profiles that a piece on Romney would be entertaining and interesting—and so he persevered. "I figured, hell, if the boss is skeptical, then I'll show the boss how wrong he is," Mike explains. "So we spent a couple of months with Mitt, and they were stunned at the quality of this individual. We even got into his Mormonism. He is very interesting."

CHARACTERS. Another big part of finding good stories is identifying the characters through which to tell them. Characters drive much of good journalism, particularly feature stories. "Making your subjects characters who are as interesting for how they talk, in what setting, and what they look like as for what they say is what makes stories memorable," explains Kim Murphy. It's the same in television. "I find a person who will be the centerpiece, or a large part of the story. It's essential to choose the right person," explains Lin Garlick. She usually finds the main character by doing short interviews with a few people directly involved in a story she's covering. She listens to them speak, gauges their ability to tell their story in their own words, and then usually picks the one who's the most natural. "Not necessarily the one who had played the biggest part in the story. I go for the ones who themselves had a story to tell," Garlick explains.

Pelley says he's often approached by young producers on his staff with ideas for stories that not only are too general but also lack the necessary focus on central characters. "They come in my office and they say, 'Climate change! It's huge!' And I send them back out the door and I say, 'That's an issue. That's a very important issue. But it's not a story. You go find a story about climate change and we'll talk. I tell them that Steven Spielberg did not do a movie called *The Holocaust*. He did a movie called *Schindler's List*. It was about the Holocaust, covered the Holocaust beginning to end. But it was about this one guy and his factory and his people. Spielberg didn't do a movie called *D-Day*. He did a movie called *Saving Private Ryan*. It was about D-Day, but he told that entire D-Day epic through the story of this one individual. And that's the difference. And that's something that a lot of young people don't quite get. If you have an issue that you want to address, that's the first step, but the second, hugely important step is to find the story that you can tell about that issue, that illuminates the issue and makes it something that the audience really wants to know about." He says that's why his story about the oncology clinic in Las Vegas shutting down due to the financial crisis was so good—because it told the issue through the story of the people who were really affected. And many of Pelley's best stories—in fact, journalism's best stories—do the same thing.

In journalism it is simpler to sound off than it is to find out.
It is more elegant to pontificate than it is to sweat.

—SIR HAROLD EVANS, journalist and author

Research

Once you have the idea for a story, the next step is to research it thoroughly. That sounds easy, but often it's not. It's easy to think you've done enough research when you haven't. Researching is like peeling away layers of an onion—there's often another layer underneath. The best researchers dig and dig until they know almost as much about a topic as the people involved in it directly. Scott Pelley says there are three keys to the successful story: "Preparation, preparation, preparation."

He says that by the time he does a story, he knows almost as much about it as the people he'll be interviewing.

As you do your research, you'll start looking for answers to the basic questions your story will need to answer. Virtually every journalism textbook will name six questions as the central ones that every piece of journalism must answer: *Who? What? Where? Why? When? How?* These questions, termed "the five Ws and an H," are the foundations of most news reporting. But we suggest two more: *So what? What's next?* The *so what* answers the question "Why should I care?" It reminds reporters to focus on impact and significance. That's very important, and not necessarily something that will be covered by the other questions. The *what's next* helps keep the audience focused on the fact that the story isn't necessarily over just because you're reporting about it. It often helps keep people on the lookout for developments in the future, or at least to keep them looking for more news. That adds up to eight questions every good piece of journalism must answer.

The usual first step in researching is to dig up other articles written about the subject—ones that help you answer the basic questions you'll need to cover in your story. We'll usually compile dozens of articles about each subject to try to educate ourselves to a high degree before jumping into a story. The longer you have to prepare, the more you can do. If you've got to do an interview right away for a breaking news story, you may have only enough time to get the basics of the story. But before a major interview, you may spend hours preparing. Mike had the luxury of spending days combing through research before a *60 Minutes* interview—reading everything he could find about the topic, and looking at prior interviews done by his potential interview subjects.

The Internet has made this aspect of researching stories

much, much easier than ever before, to the extent that young journalists often feel that *all* research can be done on the Internet. That's just not the case. The Internet is a great starting point, but if the point of your story is to break new ground, you have to speak with people who know the subject. The best way to research a story, Anderson says, is the same method that worked twenty or forty years ago: "Approach people who are involved in the story, who know about certain aspects of the story, and plumb them for what the facts are, or what the truth is." We can't emphasize this enough: if you really want to come up with new information instead of a rehash of existing information, you simply must get out and speak with the people involved.

The central dilemma in journalism is that you don't know what you don't know.

—BOB WOODWARD, journalist and author

Finding Interview Subjects

The research process is meant to give you sufficient background to understand the subject you're covering—but it should also help you identify the people to interview for the story. Again, Internet research is a good first step in determining whom to interview for a story, but it's only the first step. For one thing, the Internet will help you find people who have *already* spoken on a subject—but a good reporter also uncovers new people to interview who may have new information. The best way to do that is have your sources suggest other people to interview. "Usually talking to one person will give you three more names, and the list expands exponentially, until you feel, 'Okay, now I've got it,'" explains Anderson. Remember that you may interview a person to put his or her quotes into your story, but you may also interview someone simply for background. Reporters often speak with people just to deepen their understanding of a topic.

Picking interview subjects is an area where the amount of lead time you have and the type of story you're doing start to make a difference. If you're working on a medium-length or long story and have several days or more to work, you have a distinct advantage. Longer story length means that you can interview more people and include more information from each person in your report. But if you're working on a breaking story or have little time until you must produce your story, it gets a lot harder to get hold of the key interview subjects. Journalists who work at places such as websites and morning news shows often must compromise because of time constraints and interview someone who may not be the central character in a particular story but has enough knowledge to be credible. It's still usually better to interview a less-than-perfect subject than to interview no one at all, providing the person you do find to interview is in fact knowledgeable about the matter at hand.

Lining up interview subjects may sometimes require a fight. When news is breaking, multiple news organizations often want to speak with the same key newsmakers. Some people, usually government officials such as the secretary of state, actually can make the rounds of every major morning news show when there's a big story. The official may sit in front of a camera that is being fed out to ABC, CBS, CNN, Fox, and NBC, and do an interview with each station in turn. But it's more likely that a fight will break out among the networks over who gets the key guest on a breaking news story. "There's an incredible amount of competition, especially in morning TV," explains Russ Mitchell, who spent thirteen years anchoring the morning news at CBS. He says that NBC's *Today*, which is the highest in the ratings, tends to have the easiest time securing "gets"—the most sought-after guests—leaving *The Early Show* and ABC's *Good Morning America* in a less desirable position. "There are times when we get the 'get' because they like the booker, they like the broadcast, they like the person interviewing them. But I have to tell you, it's disheartening to see another network land the big, obvious 'get' that morning. So it's become very important in the process, and it's pretty cutthroat." One of the biggest "gets" of recent years was the first interview with Monica Lewinsky, the young woman who had an affair with President Bill Clinton. After considering numerous offers, Lewinsky chose Barbara Walters of ABC News, no doubt because she thought Walters would be sympathetic to her side of the story. But there is a "get" to be gotten almost every day.

THE RELUCTANT INTERVIEWEE. Of course, not everyone likes to speak with journalists. Mike has been extraordinarily lucky in that many people at the top of their fields felt that being interviewed by him was like a rite of passage—tangible proof that they had made it to the acme of their profession. "A crook doesn't feel like he's made it until he's been on *60 Minutes*," Mike likes to say, quoting his colleague Morley Safer. But some potential interview subjects are downright hostile, or afraid, and take convincing. This is a subject that Mike also knows well, as many of the people he interviewed had to be persuaded to sit down with him.

There's a bit of an art to convincing the reluctant interviewee. The best tactic is simply to tell the person that she'll be better off if she presents her side of the story or her side of the issue. "The obvious pitch to them is, 'But we want to get your side of this,'" Robert Anderson says. "'We're not hostile to you. We're inquisitive. We want to know what your view of this is.'" That's clearly a tactic that works as well for a journalist starting off as it does for someone at *60 Minutes*. Almost everyone appreciates balance, and almost everyone would like the chance to tell her side of a story. Chris Wallace says that although his show has bookers who convince guests to come on, he sometimes gets personally involved in persuading a guest to appear. "It's not unusual at all for me to try to close an interview, to try to close the agreement to do the interview, to express my own personal interest. Sometimes I call the politician or policy maker; sometimes I call their chief of staff to raise the level of interest to a higher level," says Wallace. "My feeling is that the most important thing on a Sunday talk show is the guest. I'd much rather do a B job with an A guest than an A job with a B guest."

And Wallace, like many other journalists, isn't above playing hardball to get the guests he wants. In the lead-up to the election of 2008, there was one candidate whom Wallace just couldn't seem to land for his Fox show—Barack Obama. "Really ever since he was elected in 2004, but especially since he started running in late 2007, we had tried to get him on," Wallace says. "I had called his office, his campaign office, not every week but often, and they kept saying, 'Oh, it's going to happen, it's going to happen,' and at a certain point it became clear to me it *wasn't* going to happen. And so we thought, well, how do we up the ante? And we came up with the idea of the Obama Watch." Wallace borrowed the digital clock from the Fox show *24* and put it on the screen—counting back from a date in 2006 when Obama first promised Wallace an interview. "So using that as a start date, we said that it had been six hundred fifty-seven days since he had promised to do an interview, and we ran the clock every week—the number of days, the number of hours, the number of minutes, the number of seconds, and started this Obama Watch," Wallace explains. "And we did it for about four weeks, and finally they called and said, 'Okay, you got him.' So there are all kinds of ways to book a guest."

On the other hand, some people who perhaps shouldn't agree to interviews do so. That's proof that asking someone for an interview sometimes brings results, even though you think the person you want to speak with won't agree. Mike has gotten more than his fair share of interviews in this category, such as pitcher Roger Clemens. Clemens sat down for what was to be Mike's last piece for *60 Minutes* in January 2008, after fresh and well-substantiated allegations that Clemens had used anabolic steroids, which are banned by Major League Baseball. Clemens was flooded with interview requests. "Everyone was calling them," recalls Anderson, who produced the Clemens piece for *60 Minutes*. Mike's advantage was that he had interviewed Clemens once before, and Clemens had liked the piece. "They felt we'd be fair," says Anderson. "They felt that Roger would be able to make the points that he wanted to make and withstand cross examination at the highest level, thereby adding to his credibility. That was the hope." Press reports at the time concluded that Clemens did not end up convincing many people of his innocence, but he certainly did get a chance to argue his case in detail, as he answered all the tough questions Mike fired at him. Mike says that Clemens accomplished what he set out to do. "He came to play. From the moment he started to answer, I realized what he was doing. He went, 'Hey, you don't believe me? Okay, I'm gonna handle this head-on. Give me every tough question imaginable and I'll answer it.' "

TO AMBUSH OR NOT TO AMBUSH? And sometimes an interviewee is so reluctant that he won't agree to an interview request at all, meaning the only way to talk is by doing an ambush. In the previous chapter, we explained Mike's reluctance to do ambush interviews—too much heat and not enough light, meaning they produce too much drama and not enough useful information. But there were some times where an ambush was critical—as with a 1993 report about abuse by priests in New Mexico. For years before the report, parents had filed dozens of complaints and later lawsuits alleging that priests had molested their children, both boys and girls. Archbishop Robert Sanchez of New Mexico ignored the complaints. "Whenever a parishioner complained, the archbishop said, 'Whoa, this is the first I have ever heard about this,' and moved the priest to another parish without warning the new parishioners that this guy had a tainted past," explains Anderson, who produced that report. Mike and his team couldn't get access to the archbishop, not even to ambush him, but they did manage to find Father Robert Kirsch, a close friend of the archbishop who was accused of and later admitted having sexual relations with a fifteen-year-old girl. Kirsch was on a pilgrimage, walking through the hills of New Mexico, when Mike, Anderson, and their crew ambushed him. Mike asked him why this young girl was claiming she had been coerced into having relations with Kirsch. "He wasn't about to answer the question, but it gave us an opportunity to use the questions, so it helped us tell the story," Mike recalls. "It gives you the opportunity to put the questions on the record, and him *not* answering tells a hell of a story." Anderson remembers having a debate with Mike beforehand about whether an ambush was called for. "I said, 'Let's not reveal that we are here,'" says Anderson. "And Mike said, 'To hell with that. We have this priest here and now. Let's find out what he has to say.' And in retrospect it was pretty obvious that Mike was right." Just before *60 Minutes* ran Mike's story, the archbishop resigned—a move that was interpreted as an admission of guilt. Afterward, dozens of lawsuits were filed against the archdiocese by those abused by pedophile priests, and the archdiocese and its insurers paid out millions of dollars in settlements.

Legitimate news shows such as *60 Minutes* still do ambushes, but according to staff at the show, they are done for information, not just drama—for light, not just heat. But ambush interviews are also still being done at some places for heat. Bill O'Reilly of Fox News Channel has his producers ambush interview subjects on a regular basis. O'Reilly defends the ambushes and says they're only meant to confront people who won't answer questions about the things they do. "Now, some object to displays like these," O'Reilly admits. "But we feel they're a vital tool in holding public servants accountable for their actions, and we do not go after people lightly. We always ask them on the program first, or to issue a clear statement explaining their actions." But several of the ambush victims say they were never invited on the show beforehand. The point of the ambushes on *The O'Reilly Factor* seems to us to be to create dramatic television, not really to get answers.

INTERVIEW ORDER. The sequence in which you interview people is also important. If you're doing a short story or a breaking news report, you simply try to get whomever you can, as soon as you can. But if you're doing a long-form piece or investigative story, then you need to strategize about the order in which you should do your interviews. Usually you start with less important characters and then end with the major characters, so that you have the maximum amount of information at your disposal when it comes time for the key interviews. This technique is used particularly effectively by prize-winning author Bob Woodward, who broke the Watergate scandal and now mainly writes books about what really goes on inside the White House. "Woodward starts with the lowest-ranking people to find out as much as he can about whatever topic he is researching, and then he works his way up the totem pole," explains Anderson. "And as he gets to the higher rungs, they realize, 'Gee, he really knows a lot of this stuff. I want to make sure he doesn't misinterpret what he knows and paint me in a bad light.'" So people talk to Woodward to protect themselves. And that's a tactic young journalists can employ. If you do a lot of work and gather a lot of information, it makes it more likely that the person you're focusing on will want to put his thoughts on the record, too. Speaking to people's underlings is one way to do that. Speaking to their bosses and even their competitors can also do wonders to get people to agree to be interviewed.

The proper question isn't what a journalist thinks is relevant but what his or her audience thinks is relevant.

—MICHAEL KINSLEY, journalist and author

Preparing for the Interview

Before sitting down across from your subject, it's important to write down a list of questions and to strategize for the interview itself. This part of the process can really make a difference in how your interview pans out. Mike's son Chris says that one of the most important things he learned from his dad was to never walk into an interview unprepared. "You're almost necessarily going to be interviewing somebody who knows more about the subject than you do. If you're interviewing a movie star, they know a lot more about their movie and their craft than you do. If I'm interviewing the president's economic advisor, I certainly hope he knows more about economics than I do," says Wallace. "All of which is to say that if you want to get someone off his talking points, if you want to get him off his script, you've got to know enough that you can challenge him." Wallace not only does in-depth research but even plays out possible scenarios for questions and answers. "If I ask the person this, what are they going to say and how do I respond to that? I think those are absolutely key to doing a successful interview." Wallace calls this practice "war gaming," and it's a great way to help you prepare for a big interview.

That's why many if not most professional journalists go into interviews with a list of questions. Some experienced journalists may go in with only a list of topics to cover, without specific questions, especially if they're beat reporters who cover the same topic day in and day out, but some game plan of this sort is absolutely essential. Especially if you're new to journalism, you should plan out your interviews to ensure you get all the information you need to do your story properly—not just the details but also the more important questions of *why* and *so what*.

As Mike points out, the very process of writing questions helps ensure that you're ready for the interview. "What I used to do was to get a yellow legal pad and write down fifty questions.

In putting together those questions, you are educating yourself. You're doing your own research," he says. The better your research, the better the questions you're able to write. "You may discard all fifty questions, but because you've done that kind of research ahead of time, enough to write fifty questions, you've familiarized yourself with the subject and are ready for whatever happens."

That's why we advise young journalists to prepare a long and detailed list of questions for each person they interview. But in fact, that list of questions is just a starting point for the interview. As we'll discuss in detail in the next chapter, just as important as the questions you prepare in advance are the *follow-up questions* you ask based on what someone actually tells you during the interview. So yes, a good journalist has to be willing to stray from the script, but having a list of solid questions in front of you helps make sure you're prepared. It can also be helpful if the interview starts to stall. "You may jettison all—maybe not all, but maybe forty of the questions," Mike explains. "But if the interview isn't going anyplace after the first ten questions or whatever, then you can look back down at your yellow pad and say, 'Oh, yeah, let's ask that one.' That helps restart the interview."

Questions also need to be phrased in the right way. Good journalists almost always ask their questions in a way that invites a long answer. The best way to do that is by asking what are called *open-ended questions*, ones that cannot be answered with a simple yes or no. They invite the interview subject to speak at length. Journalists should use *closed-ended questions*, which are specific in nature and invite short answers, sparingly. A closed-ended question might be "Did you tell the truth when you said you never took steroids?" The answer can only be yes or no. An open-ended question might be "How did you feel when you were first accused of taking steroids?" It's a question that invites a long answer, and it's more likely than the closed-ended question to provide an interesting quote. You usually find both kinds of questions in the typical interview—but you have to learn when each is warranted. "Don't ask questions that give the interviewee a choice, such as 'Were you at the scene of the accident, or did you arrive after it had happened?'" adds our CBS News colleague Elizabeth Palmer. "Your phrasing will box them in. Make the interviewee work at an answer with a more general question—for example, 'When did you arrive on the scene?' Very occasionally, if you're really trying to pin someone on something extremely specific, it's okay to ask a yes-or-no question, but usually it gives the interviewee an easy out. Better to force them to give full information by asking *how*, *where*, *when*, or *why* questions." If you watch highly experienced journalists conduct interviews, you'll find that they tend to do it exactly that way.

In terms of phrasing, keep your questions short and sweet. Scott Pelley of *60 Minutes* says a good question ought to be no longer than six words. "I think questions should be very brief and direct and straight to the point, and that gets a much more honest answer out of people instead of letting people think about it and think about it and think about it as you unroll this thirty-second question," he says. "It's a very common mistake that people make." Chris Wallace agrees that a short and focused question increases your chance of getting a useful answer. "I believe that the longer and more convoluted the question, the more opportunity you give the guest to get off on a side-track, to avoid the point of your question. So I think it's really key to hone it down," Wallace says. "Remove all the fat and all the subordinate clauses, and keep it as straight and focused as it can be."

Wallace also recommends a technique in that vein taught to him by longtime NBC News anchor Tom Brokaw—just ask, "What do you think of . . . ?" It's a technique Wallace has used many times to great effect, including once with British prime minister Margaret Thatcher. "I was the host of the *Today* show in 1982, and it was the time of the Israeli invasion of Lebanon, and the Brits and U.S. were very upset with Israel," he explains. Thatcher was hard to interview because she had been so finely honed by all the debates in British politics that she'd developed a computer-like ability to analyze a question, explains Wallace, so he looked for a way to break through her defenses and get her real opinion of the Israeli prime minister. "I said to her, 'What do you think of Menachem Begin?' It was so quick and so simple that you can't get out of it. Anything you say, even any pause in how you say it, says something. She started for a second, like, 'Wow, how do I answer that one?' because, clearly, what she really thought of Menachem Begin at that particular moment was that he was a pain in the neck," Wallace said. "I set her back, just for a second, but it gave me great satisfaction."

Good questions should also show that you've done your homework, but in a subtle way. There's no reason to quote back word for word a speech someone made or an article he may have written, just to prove you're prepared. It's better if the amount of work you've put in becomes evident from the depth of your questions. You could say to someone, "On August thirteenth, 2004, in a speech to the National Association of University Presidents, you said that, quote, 'Universities are finding they have more opportunities than ever before to recruit students from outside the United States, and we should all do so.' Why?" That's okay, but your interviewee already knows what he said when he gave a speech, and you can assume he remembers what he said. Instead, just ask, "You've been urging other colleges to recruit more foreign students. Why?" Referring to his quote this way still shows you've done your homework, but it gets you to the question you want to ask quickly and simply.

3

THE TALK: THE ART OF THE INTERVIEW

Great questions make great reporting.

—DIANE SAWYER, journalist

Interviewing is the lifeblood of journalism. *Every* story, whether hard or soft news, print, Internet, or broadcast, depends on interviews. That means that mastering the art of the interview is critical. Make no mistake: interviewing *is* an art, one learned over many years of journalistic work. While some people are inherently better interviewers than others, all journalists are constantly refining their interview techniques.

What is a good interview to Mike Wallace, the master of the form? "An interview is good if it brings you information that you had no ken of before," Mike says. "An interview is good if the interviewer feels that he or she has succeeded in this voyage of discovery." A good interview, in other words, gives you the new information you need to do a great story.

Of course, on radio or television, interviews take on an added dimension. They're not only for information—they're also a performance. "An interview is good if the reaction on camera of the interviewee is such that it pierces that phony façade of somebody hiding behind his or her answer with a non-informative answer," Mike explains. Television journalists such as Mike thrive on that moment where the camera captures the piercing of the façade—but that moment is really the goal for every journalist, camera or no camera. Interview subjects nowadays are usually well prepared for the questioning they get from journalists. That means journalists have to be better prepared than ever to make sure an interview goes well and cuts to the heart of the matter at hand.

The Nature of Interviews

Most journalism textbooks say that a good interview is akin to a conversation. Beth teaches as much in her classes at Fordham. But Mike doesn't buy it. "A conversation can go a million different ways," he says. "A conversation is aimless." He sees interviews in a whole different light. To him, interviews are a *negotiation*. The person doing the interview wants something. The person being interviewed also wants something. Each interview is a battle of wits in which both parties set out to get what they desire. So when you are preparing for an interview, don't just think about what information *you* need. "Look at it from the point of view of the person being interviewed," Mike advises. "The fact that they are willing to sit down with you means they respect you. And they want the audience that you are going to be able to deliver." Imagine the calculus that's going on inside the mind of your interview subject. Then try to use that to your advantage.

A perfect example of the interview as negotiation is Mike's 2008 interview with Roger Clemens, which (as we've discussed) was a classic case of someone trying to stand up to the most intense possible scrutiny. Clemens wanted to prove his innocence, and Mike, who was eighty-nine at the time, wanted to show his bosses at CBS that he could still land and pull off the big interviews. Mike had interviewed Clemens once before, in 2001. "I went down to interview him at his home in Texas, and I was astonished to find that he was unlike a lot of sports figures or sports stars. He was articulate; he was in a strange way gentle, very close to his mother; cared a great bit about what people felt and thought about him," Mike recalls. "He watched *60 Minutes*. He was a fan of sorts. He saw the kind of thing that we did. He realized that he had nothing in the world to hide. That was the beginning of the relationship, and by the time we got through we had become friends. Not close friends, of course, but he trusted us." Although he and Clemens had not stayed in touch afterward, Mike thinks that that first interview was the key to getting the second. After the Mitchell Report about steroid use in baseball came out, "Clemens said, 'Yeah, I'll be happy to sit down with Mike because I know him, he knows me, we can trust each other,'" Mike says.

For Mike, it was a golden opportunity, not only to obtain what journalists call the "get"—the hottest, most desirable interview possible—but also to ask his subject absolutely anything. "Here is a guy that trusts us. Here is a guy that is in trouble with the public, who is being treated very skeptically by a lot of sports reporters. What a wonderful opportunity to really go after this guy," Mike says. "We could ask him anything and he would answer anything. We were free to ask him any question that he wanted, and he sat down knowing that we were going to ask him tough stuff." It was a rare level of trust and cooperation.

And Mike says that Clemens rose to the occasion, despite the tough questions. "From the moment that I sat down, I realized that he could be his own best witness. He said, 'You got tough stuff? Throw it at me. I'll answer it for you. I believe in myself and there is no reason why the public should not believe in me, too.'" Mike doesn't know if Clemens was telling the truth or not, but he thinks Clemens did a creditable job of defending himself.

It was because Mike knew what was going through Clemens' head when he agreed to the interview that he was able to unload his toughest questions on the star—and create the highest-rated episode of *60 Minutes* in over three years.

I try to get people to forget the lights and the cameras and just talk to me as if we were alone in the room.

—BARBARA WALTERS, journalist and author

Establishing Rapport

The key to successful interviews is rapport. That's why reporters don't usually jump right into their interviews, unless it's with an official who is pressed for time. They usually chat a bit before the formal part of the interview, as a way of establishing some common ground with the person being interviewed. That bond may come from a shared sense of purpose in getting the interview done, from having mutual friends, or from some kind of shared interest. Building that sense of rapport is often the difference between a good interview and a great interview.

One way to build rapport is to bring up any friends or acquaintances you have in common with the subject, as you're chatting before getting to your questions. "You say, 'Oh, by the way, individuals A, B, C, and D are friends of mine, and they have told me how much they admire you,' or 'They have a couple of questions they want me to ask you,'" says Mike. "That is bound to stimulate interest in the interviewee. Or you say, 'I must say, you certainly do have some people that are skeptical about you. And I've talked to some of them. And I'm sure that you'll want to answer some of the things that they have told me to ask you.'" Any other thing that builds common ground is good. Perhaps you and your subject come from the same area, or attended the same school, or share the same hobby. Deep research often turns up these kinds of points of commonality.

Another way to build rapport, especially if there is no obvious common interest, is just to get the subject talking. Mike sometimes does that by asking the interview subject about something in the news that day. "Did you hear about, and what is your reaction to, something that is at the top of the news?" Even such a simple question will begin the process of building rapport.

If you can't find some common ground in your research, then find something your interviewee is passionate about. "I'll usually try to interview someone in his or her office, where there will be something personal, like a photograph or a piece of art," explains Beth. "People usually love to talk about themselves, and so there will almost always be something on display that can spark a conversation." Family pictures, awards, books, or knickknacks work well as conversation starters.

But sometimes nothing works. Then what do you do? If the conversation isn't flowing, Mike usually just calls his interview subject on the carpet. "Look," Mike will explain, "I'm trying to find out about you. I can't get it from yes, no, or maybe. I have to believe that you are trying to communicate with me, just as

I am trying to communicate with you. So let's settle down and try to find out about each other." A softer version of that might work for beginning reporters. There's nothing wrong with saying to a source, "I wonder if you might make your answers a bit longer, or a bit more detailed, so that I get more information. I really don't know much about this, and really appreciate your assistance." That's not sucking up—it's just a way to help make an interview go well.

Sometimes the rapport between a reporter and source comes naturally, as it did in 2004 when Mike interviewed Fox News Channel star Bill O'Reilly. "I think that he respected my work," posits Mike. Whether he had agreed with it or not, he respected what I had done. So it was easy to begin to talk to him." Of course, it's not hard to imagine two of television's top personalities getting along well. A much more difficult person to bond with was Iranian president Mahmoud Ahmadinejad. "He knew who the dickens I was, Ahmadinejad did," Mike says. "So he was ready. And he knew the reputation of *60 Minutes*. He wanted to take advantage of it and was willing to entertain difficult questions or controversial or confrontational ones. And I think he enjoyed it." Mike thought he was able to build some rapport with Ahmadinejad because they both wanted the interview to succeed. "He wanted the American people to see him in action," says Mike.

Something about the television process also helps build rapport, because doing a television interview is complicated and expensive, and shows a certain seriousness. "This is an important undertaking, obviously, to me, the interviewer. And the interviewee is bound to know it, and the people around him are bound to know it. It's not just flattery," Mike explains. "The fact that all of this is going on, I mean, this costs money. This costs time." If the subject stops to think how much effort went into setting up and preparing for the interview, it may encourage him or her to give thoughtful, serious answers.

But even in a TV interview, sometimes you're simply unable to create much rapport. During Mike's 1979 interview with Ayatollah Khomeini, the spiritual leader of Iran, the ayatollah simply didn't look at him. "That said so much, the fact that he wouldn't look at me," recalls Mike. "He had agreed to sit down with this character, this interviewer. Why did he sit down with me? His people apparently felt that it was a good idea for him, for them." Yet the ayatollah's people could not force their boss to make eye contact with Mike. The lack of rapport, the lack of eye contact, became part of the story. The image in America of the ayatollah as a cruel and cold ruler was only enhanced by the way he appeared during Mike's interview.

Russ Mitchell, anchor for CBS News, recalls some interviews where the rapport didn't materialize, and when you're on live television, that is a major problem. "I was interviewing Jewel, the singer, who really had nothing to say. And I had four minutes to talk to her. And about a minute into it, it was clear she didn't want to be there. She had just 'written' this book but knew nothing about the book. And as I'm asking her questions, she's actually not answering anything—she's being rather snippy, actually—and I just said, 'Jewel, you gotta work with me. We've got four minutes to go,'" Mitchell says with a chuckle. "And she started laughing and she got better."

And then again, rapport can also go totally the other way. Sometimes an interviewer and his or her subject get along so well that their rapport morphs into flirtation. Some journalists flirt unabashedly. In teaching about the career of ABC News star Barbara Walters, for example, Beth has her students watch footage in which Walters acts flirtatiously with many men, including actors, foreign leaders, and American presidents. And Mike has no problem with doing the same thing. "Sometimes you want to flirt with either attractive women or older women who want to be flirted with," he says. "You want to get the best out of your interviewee that you can get by whatever means." Beth covered professional sports in Russia and can clearly remember fighting the urge to flirt with some of the world's most successful tennis, hockey, and basketball players—especially during the National Hockey League lockout in 2005, when some of the NHL's best players came to play in Moscow, and she had to interview them in various stages of undress in their locker room.

A journalist's gender or race can also be a factor in establishing rapport. Barbara Walters is a master of using her gender to her advantage, whether she is being flirtatious with a man or creating the feeling of being girlfriends when talking with a woman. And our late, great CBS News colleague Ed Bradley was able to create a special bond with other African Americans. "He had the advantage—this is going to sound crazy—he had the advantage of being black," says Mike about Bradley. Of all his many reports, Bradley used to say he was most proud of a 1983 interview he did with the singer Lena Horne, who also was black. Although she was sixty-four and he just forty-two, they had an on-camera chemistry that sizzled, and Horne said that their shared race was one reason why they bonded so strongly. "That was a superb interview," says Mike. "He got a lot of stuff out of her that no one else I know could. I wouldn't be able to get that out of her." Bradley did hundreds of marvelous stories for *60 Minutes*, but some of those that stand out to us involved other African Americans: singer Ray Charles, golfer Tiger Woods, and boxer Muhammad Ali. Other reporters agree that their race or gender can sometimes be helpful. "When I reported stories about court-ordered busing, whites would tell me things that they would not tell me if I were black and vice versa simply because, being Asian, I had no tribe," explains Anthony Ramirez, a Filipino American whose career has included assignments at several national newspapers.

Establishing lasting rapport is a process that doesn't end when the journalist closes her notebook or turns off his recorder. It's almost always a good idea to make sure that the lines of communication stay open after an interview is done. You start this process as soon as the formal part of the interview ends. A good reporter doesn't just get up and leave, unless he or she senses that the interview subject is pressed for time. It's usually a good idea to chat for a moment before getting up to go. You may want to ask the person you've interviewed if there's anything you forgot to ask about or anything the subject would like to add. Another good idea: ask the person you've interviewed how best to get back in touch in case you have questions or need additional information. You may want to ask for a cell phone number or an e-mail address at which you can reach the source again. Some people feel uncomfortable asking for personal information, but it's far better to ask than to need more information come deadline and have no way to reach your interviewee. Accuracy serves them as well as you.

And it's never a bad idea to send some kind of note thanking the subject for his or her time. In the age of e-mail, it's now particularly easy to send off a two- or three-line note. It doesn't have to gush—you just need to let the person you interviewed know that you appreciate his or her time. You want to make sure the door stays open to future interviews, and perhaps even to developing a professional relationship with the person you've interviewed. If the rapport is good, that person you've interviewed may become a valuable long-term source.

My basic approach to interviewing is to ask the basic questions that might even sound naive, or not intellectual. Sometimes when you ask the simple questions like "Who are you?" or "What do you do?" you learn the most.

—BRIAN LAMB, founder, C-SPAN

Interviewing Styles

There are countless techniques for doing an interview and establishing rapport. Mike's usual persona might be called the Grand Inquisitor, but even he has a variety of techniques that he calls upon during his interviews. He may tone things down like a kindly uncle, or dial them up like a stern judge. He says the choice of style depends on the focus of the report. "Is this interview for fact, for political reaction, for emotional reaction?" he asks. "And if that's on your mind when you go into an interview, then you write the questions in such a way ahead of time."

In other words, the tone of your questions will vary from interview to interview according to the subject. If you're interviewing someone about a serious disease she has, for instance, it's probably inappropriate to be accusatory or pushy. The style of the interview may also vary depending on whether it will be broadcast live, will be used later in a print or broadcast piece, or is simply for background and will not be quoted directly at all.

We've seen a variety of different styles work very effectively for different correspondents. They tend to range from know-it-all to total simpleton, from judge to co-conspirator. In fact, interview style really depends on your own personality. It's hard to appear to be someone you're not. The most famous interviewers in America have all developed their own unique styles. As we've discussed, Barbara Walters is a master at creating a conspiratorial bond with her interview subjects—befriending and cajoling them into revealing themselves. She's sympathetic and empathetic, and people sit down with her because they know she'll be kind to them. Former ABC News anchor Ted Koppel's style is completely different. He doesn't try to make friends with his interview subjects. In fact, when he hosted *Nightline*, Koppel's guests were usually seated in another studio, even if they were located in the same city as Koppel. This created distance between interviewer and interviewee, helping Koppel ask tough, fact-based questions.

Personal interview styles take a long time to develop; it's really a matter of experience, and of trial and error. But one good guideline is to try to be true to your own personality. If you're a sweet natured person, it's unlikely that you'll turn into a tiger when doing interviews.

BASIC TECHNIQUES. Lots of different interview techniques work very effectively, but there are a few that are particularly useful for young reporters. There's what we call the "aw-shucks school of interviewing," where you pretend you don't know much about your subject matter. You make people start at the beginning and walk you slowly and carefully through a story. You might tell your interview subject, "You know, I don't know much about that. Could you please explain it to me simply, and from the beginning? Pretend that I'm your grandfather and walk me through everything." In fact, you may actually know quite a bit about the subject, but this technique ensures that you'll get a lot of information from the person you're interviewing, and will get the whole story. This is a great technique to make sure that people simplify complicated things.

Then there's a technique we call *repeating*. You repeat things back to make sure you've understood. "Let me see if I have this right," you can say, and then repeat essential information. That's really useful when the information you're getting is very complex.

Remember that sometimes a reporter's youth or inexperience can actually be an asset. "The very innocence of the young interviewer is in his or her favor," Mike says. Beth can say after advising the Fordham newspaper, and having been a student reporter herself once, that interview subjects are likely to give a young journalist some leeway. And if a student or a beginner comes into an interview well prepared, having done his or her research well, with a list of pertinent and well-thought-out questions, then an interviewee will often bend over backward to try to be helpful.

HOW TO ASK THE TOUGH QUESTIONS. Learning to ask the hard questions is one of the most difficult things for beginning journalists to master, but it's also one of the most important. Inexperienced journalists tend to worry that the person they're interviewing will get angry with them if the questions get too hard. "Perhaps they will," says Mike. "But if you are smart as an interviewer, you won't ask it in such a way as to let the interviewee get mad." Mike says that the key is to be deferential—and to back up your questions with evidence. "You pick up something and show them and say, 'You know what it says here,'" Mike explains. "Immediately the interviewee knows where the question is coming from, what has triggered it.'"

More important, young reporters ought not to worry about how they will be judged by their interview subjects. Building rapport with your subject is important, yes, but you can't let it get in the way of getting the information you seek. Ultimately, this isn't a popularity contest. You have a job to do.

Of course, being tough can be hard to do if you're, say, a student journalist and will have to face a certain professor or dean over and over again. Or if you get a chance to interview a movie star whose work you really love. But you sell yourself short if you shy away from tough questions. "If you are with the object of your inquiry and you have the opportunity to do it, go for it! If it triggers anger, what have you lost?" asks Mike. Even if you have to ask a tough question of someone you need to interview again, the interview subject will probably respect you more for being brave enough to ask the tough questions, as long as those questions are asked politely and are based on good research. When we think about asking hard questions, we remember the saying "There is no such thing as an indiscreet question." Everyone who is famous or holds power is fair game for an indiscreet or tough question.

Every journalist has his or her way of asking the tough question. Barbara Walters does it by almost apologizing first, saying something like, "I really hate to ask this, but everyone wants to know . . ." or "I know this may be difficult for you to talk about, but . . ." Although he's been likened to a bull in a china shop when it comes to questioning his subjects, Mike actually has an arsenal of softer interviewing tools. "There are certain questions and certain expressions I use," he says. "When you are asking a tough question and you say, 'Look, forgive me for this, but . . . ,' and then you go to the tough question. Or 'Oh, come on!' which means, 'Hey, don't kid me.'"

CBS News correspondent Elizabeth Palmer is particularly skilled at asking tough questions in a polite way. She never makes them sound like a personal attack. She'll ask the tough questions, but respectfully. "Try to avoid a 'Gotcha!' or an 'I'm going to get you' tone," Palmer says. "Instead, be firmly but politely insistent until you get a good, satisfying answer to your questions. Ask a hard question several times in a row if you don't get a good answer. Simply having to repeat a question makes the point that the subject hasn't answered and is being evasive."

Her next piece of advice applies particularly well to the TV interview: "If you are asking good, tough questions in a reasonable way, your listeners and viewers will be with you and expect good answers, too. If the interviewee doesn't deliver, he or she will have lost the sympathy of the viewers. On the other hand, if you attack the interviewee, you risk making the viewers sorry for them." And that is something to avoid, as you want the audience's sympathies to remain with you, the interviewer.

ORDERING YOUR QUESTIONS. Classic journalism textbooks suggest that reporters order their questions from easiest to hardest, so that if someone gets offended by the difficult questions at the end of an interview and stops talking, the bulk of the interview has already been done. That's probably good advice for young journalists. But experienced reporters may not actually do this. Mike often asks his questions according to the mood and receptivity of the person to whom he is talking. "You work depending upon what your hunch is," he says. Yet even Mike is unlikely to rush into the heart of a matter without at least a little warm-up. And when dealing with a television interview, it's always wise to ask at least one non-crucial question at the beginning, to give the camera and sound people a chance to adjust their settings.

Of course, how you ask your questions depends on what kind of interview you're doing. When you're doing a long interview that's being taped, you usually have time to warm up the subject before getting into the meat of the story. But what if you're doing a live interview and the whole segment lasts only three minutes? CBS anchor Russ Mitchell does both long and short interviews, and he says that the ones he does live pose a particular challenge. "In this setting, you don't have time to establish any rapport. You're basically in it, and you're out of there. So what you try to do is keep your questions clear, keep the discussion conversational, and be flexible," he says. "When you're doing this short interview, listening and just trying to be nimble is the biggest attribute one can have."

FOLLOW-UP QUESTIONS. Being nimble means being able to come up with good follow-up questions—questions that come up during the course of the interview. These follow-up questions are absolutely crucial to the success of your interview. During an interview, you learn more about your subject, and your interviewee's answers often give you ideas for questions that you did not know to ask beforehand, despite your preparation. "You always go into an interview understanding that you're not going to be able to ask as many questions as you have written down, because the key is in the follow-ups," explains Scott Pelley of *60 Minutes*. "It's the questions that are *not* written down that are illuminating, where the truth gets told. It's not going to be reading question number six off the piece of paper on your lap. It's going to be in the third follow-up to question six that suddenly something's revealed."

Pelley says that the biggest skill he learned from watching Mike work was the ability to ask meaningful follow-ups. "Making somebody answer a question they don't want to answer is the end result of a series of follow-ups that back the person deeper and deeper and deeper into a corner that they can't get out of. And that's what Mike invented on television," says Pelley. "If you look at my exchange with [former CIA director George] Tenet on the subject of torture, this is an example of that. If you look at my exchange with [Iranian president] Ahmadinejad on whether he was building a nuclear weapon, this is an example of that. It's a thrust and parry—it's really more like chess, actually, than fencing, because it's a series of blocking maneuvers in which you're not allowing the subject to avoid the question, and you just block them, block them, block them until, in the final question in the series, they give up, and they give up an answer. It doesn't always work. But that's why I watched Mike's interviews, because that's what I learned."

That's why listening carefully to your interview subject is critical. Beth recalls watching a reporter she knew in Moscow conduct a television interview with a major political figure in which the reporter seemed not to listen to a thing the official said. The reporter had a list of questions on his lap and just went down the list. Because he didn't listen, the correspondent was unable to ask meaningful follow-up questions, and the interview fell flat.

It's difficult to listen carefully while taking notes and plotting your next question. It takes practice. But you can ruin an interview if you don't listen. "I think that there is a tendency among young correspondents, and producers for that matter, to have a list of questions and say, 'I want to ask one, two, three, four, five, six, seven,'" explains Russ Mitchell. "And the danger of that is at question two, the person interviewed could say, 'I shot my mom last night,' and you're saying, 'That's nice. So tell me about your latest movie.'" Remember that your question list is simply a starting point.

Sometimes the best question may not even be a question at all. With Mike, a question may be just a look—a look that says, "Really?" Ed Bradley of *60 Minutes* was also famous for using his body language to cast doubt upon what people were saying, simply by raising his eyebrows or scratching his head. Again, that's a technique that can be developed by pretty much everyone.

Newspapermen ask dumb questions.
They look up at the sun and ask if it is shining.

—SONNY LISTON, boxer

Intimidation in Interviews

It's sometimes easy for journalists to forget that being interviewed can be an intimidating experience, particularly for people who don't frequently interact with journalists. Even people who are used to speaking with reporters can get intimidated about being interviewed by a reporter with a reputation for toughness. It's been joked that the seven most intimidating words in the English language are "Mike Wallace is here to see you." "People can be afraid of talking with me," Mike admits. "People do not want to grant me the opportunity. Why? Because I have a reputation for being dishonest? I don't think so. But perhaps I can be difficult and confrontational." In the broader scheme of things, journalists can either gain or lose if they intimidate their subjects. Some people speak more when under pressure, though others clam up.

Why are some journalists particularly intimidating? Sometimes it's because the reporter's manner is brusque or cold. Or sometimes it's because the correspondent presses interview subjects hard when given less-than-truthful answers. "If you are a good interviewer, you know how to make the object of your inquiry vulnerable, because you know so much about him or her and the situation that it tears the formality away," Mike explains. In a 1993 interview with Italian opera star Luciano Pavarotti, Mike used his toughness to penetrate Pavarotti's protective shell. To do so, Mike brought up all the criticism that surrounded Pavarotti. "They said that his voice is going, he is too fat, he is lazy, his voice broke and he was booed," Mike recalls. "And I asked, 'What are you scared about? Is this the end of your career that is coming, because your throat can't carry the load as well as it did? Your voice broke when you were doing *Don Carlo* in Rome, and the people who live to go to the opera booed you.' And he said, 'Of course, they were right.' " Pavarotti then talked about his fears and failings—creating a memorable report by giving in to Mike's pressure to show his vulnerable side.

Then there are times when an interview subject tries to intimidate the interviewer. The rich and powerful are most likely to do this, but it really can happen with almost anyone. A university president might try to intimate student reporters by having them wait for a long time, or a corporate executive might do so by holding an interview in a large and impressive office. Mike remembers how Iranian president Ahmadinejad tried to intimidate him by drawing out Mike's wait for an interview. "We were in a hotel suite in Tehran, and we had been there for a long time and it was getting boring. And

Ahmadinejad had gone off to Malaysia to talk to some other Muslim leaders. And we were upset about being put off," Mike recalls. Mike, producer Robert Anderson, and the camera crew sat in Tehran and waited and waited. Ahmadinejad returned from Malaysia, and still there was no sign of any interview. "We figured that the room was bugged by the authorities in Tehran, so I remember very distinctly talking to the chandelier," says Mike. "Talking to the chandelier" is an old trick, dating back to the days of the Cold War, of talking to the walls when you are sure your room is bugged, as a way to communicate with the local authorities. So Mike finally called out to the people bugging the room, "Well, our visa runs out in about three or four days, so I guess we had better book passage on a proper plane to get back to New York." It worked. "Word came about a half hour later that he would see us," Mike explains.

Sometimes an interviewee's assistants or handlers may try to intimidate a journalist. In particular, an elected official may have a press secretary or personal assistant go speak to a reporter before an interview, to try to influence what will be asked. "Oh, no, don't ask her about that," the press secretary might say, or suggest, "She won't take any questions on that subject." Those sorts of discussions can create a very difficult situation for the reporter. The journalist has often come to talk about some piece of news, and if it's controversial, then the assistants will do their best to keep journalists away from the very nuggets of information they've come to get. Be polite but firm if you get into this kind of situation. Try to explain that your job is to ask the questions, and that the interview subject—not the handler—should be the one to decide whether to answer or not.

To me, every interview, even if you love the artist, needs to be somewhat adversarial. Which doesn't mean you need to attack the person, but you do need to look at it like you're trying to get information that has not been written about before.

—CHUCK KLOSTERMAN, journalist and author

When an Interview Turns Sour

When an interview gets off to a bad start, it can be hard to recover. Such was the case when Mike interviewed Russian president Vladimir Putin for *60 Minutes* in 2005. The interview took place at Putin's residential complex west of Moscow. The interview was scheduled for noon, and so the crews went out to the residence, Novo-Ogaryovo, early in the morning to set up. As Mike, Beth, and producer Robert Anderson got to the residence closer to the interview time, we saw Putin's motorcade pull out, heading for Moscow. "That is not a good sign," Anderson said. And he was right. It was nearly 5:00 p.m. when Putin finally showed up for the interview. And in the five hours between the time when the simultaneous translation system was set up and the president arrived, something had broken. When Mike sat in his chair and started to chat with Putin, he couldn't hear the English translation of Putin's comments. It took about ten minutes for the Russians to find the problem (luckily for Mike, Putin's staff, not CBS News people, had set up the system). During that time, Putin's impatience was clearly noticeable. It was embarrassing for Mike, even though it was not his fault. It took quite a while after that for Mike to establish the rhythm of the interview. It ended up okay, but only because it went on for more than two hours, giving Mike a chance to recover from the disastrous start.

Sometimes people are sitting down for an interview because they have to, not because they particularly want to. Under those circumstances, subjects can be sour about having to talk, and it can be hard to get them to speak candidly. Boris Yeltsin was lukewarm about giving an interview to *60 Minutes* after he left office in 2000, but we were told that he had to sit down for one American television interview after his book, *Midnight Diaries*, came out. And that one interview went to Mike. The plan was for Mike to interview Yeltsin, and then for the two men to take a golf cart for a drive around the grounds surrounding Yeltsin's house. But it didn't all come off as planned. Almost exactly one hour after the interview started, Yeltsin said, "That's it," and left. We suspected that Yeltsin was contractually obligated to a one-hour interview, and that he decided to bolt as soon as the hour was up.

During the interview, Mike did everything he could think of to win Yeltsin over. He recalls that he resorted to flattery, telling Yeltsin, "It's a pleasure and a privilege to sit down with somebody who has been a mover and a shaker in history." In an attempt to joke with Yeltsin, Mike called him "a very nice young man." None of it worked. And then Yeltsin almost walked out of the interview after half an hour because of an error made by the president's translator. Yeltsin's translator, who had been provided by the Russian government, was translating Mike's questions into Russian. A CBS News translator was translating Yeltsin's answers into English. Mike asked Yeltsin if he was "thick-skinned," meaning able to take criticism. The president's translator translated the question the wrong way—literally instead of figuratively—and asked Yeltsin if he was like a hippopotamus! Yeltsin got visibly upset and said that either there had been some error in the translation or he had gotten a totally inappropriate question and would leave. It all got worked out, but it didn't do anything to improve the atmosphere. The interview was tough going, and Mike was not impressed by Yeltsin. "I found him not as interesting, truly, as I expected," Mike says. "It was hard to take him seriously."

One of the hardest things for an interviewer to do is to draw out a reluctant interviewee, or one who is giving short or meaningless answers. Mike had to do that with one of his most famous interviews—one with Clint Hill, the Secret Service agent who was just feet from President Kennedy when he was shot. Hill, who was racked with guilt about the Kennedy assassination, agreed to sit down with Mike in 1975, but for the first hour or so of the interview he gave unrevealing answers. Mike stopped the interview and practically yelled at Hill, accusing him of spewing pabulum instead of providing real answers. Hill rallied after that and ended up spilling his guts, allowing out the emotions he had been repressing since that fateful day in 1963. Not only did it make for engrossing television, but Hill says it started a healing process that probably saved his life.

What to do in these situations? If you're an experienced reporter like Mike, you can play hardball. "Let's say that you are getting monosyllabic answers and you say, 'Come on.' In other words, 'Cut the bullshit, come on, forgive me,'" says Mike. "You are not softening them up—you're asking them to become co-conspirators with the interviewer." For a young reporter, a better tactic to use when the information is not flowing is just to be straightforward and ask the interviewee for longer and more detailed answers. Explain that you need to understand the subject inside and out, and ask him or her to walk you through the subject in a more detailed way. A smart young journalist can learn to do that in a humble manner that elicits the subject's help. And if your questions show you've done your homework, you're likely to draw out a reluctant subject.

You should also know what to do when you catch someone lying to you. It's rare, but it does happen. "I'm pretty sure a Russian governor lied to me," says Beth. "We were covering the story of a kidnapped American child and had been told by American officials that this governor had been briefed on the case in detail, since it happened in his region. So the next time this governor held a press conference, I asked him about the case, and he shocked me by saying he knew nothing about it. 'But the Americans say they briefed you,' I said. 'No, they haven't,' this official snapped back. I later went back to American officials, and they said that this man was lying. But what can you do?" It's a difficult situation for a journalist anytime it's your word against someone else's—especially when the other person is a government official. You have to have solid proof to say in print or in a broadcast that someone lied to you—and that proof can often be hard to get. If someone *is* lying, it's your job as a journalist to document that lie. But if that person is *not* lying, it's also your job to find that out for sure, to set the record straight.

If you have specific information in your possession that casts doubt on what an interview subject is saying, then bring it up in the interview. Be polite and stay factual. Say something along the lines of, "Are you sure of that? Because I see that earlier you said something else." Then quote it. Or cite the words of another person who contradicts what the subject tells you. What you want to avoid is coming right out and saying, "You're lying." Instead, ask, "How will our audience know that you're telling the truth?" This is another area in which having more experience is useful. If you have been covering a beat for a while and really know the subject, you're more likely to be able to say when someone has not been completely truthful.

WHEN YOUR SUBJECT GETS ANGRY. We've had plenty of interviews where the subjects got downright mad. Experienced journalists know that getting someone angry or upset has its benefits. "Sometime it's good when somebody gets angry, because sometimes you are going to get the truth, and sometimes that person is going to have a display that is unvarnished," says Mike.

Anger can be hard to capture in a print story. But an outburst of anger can help a written story by bringing with it information you didn't have before, such as facts that someone divulges in anger, or new insights that you get into the person's character. To capture the emotional outburst, quote the angry person extensively in your print article, to document exactly what your interview subject said. You may also cite your questions in the story, if that helps explain why the interview subject got ticked off.

Anger does play better in a television interview than in a print interview, because the audiovisual medium is better able to capture the emotion. Take, for instance, Mike's 1991 interview with actress Barbra Streisand. Mike had known Streisand since the 1950s, when she was just breaking into show business. Streisand thought that gave Wallace an unfair advantage. "I had spoken to her mother ahead of time and her mother had told me, 'Hey, Barbra doesn't have time for anybody.' And when I put that to Barbra, almost immediately she said, 'Did she say time for anybody or time for her?' And I said, 'No, she said Barbra has no time for anybody. She's basically selfish and self-absorbed. Somebody would say a self-obsessed person,'" Mike recalls. "And when that hit, you could see on her face how upset Barbra was. Then all of a sudden she began to cry." In the final piece, to his credit, Mike showed how Streisand got mad at him for the question, and how she accused him of unfair tactics. The story brought heat as Streisand got angry, but it also brought light as Mike delved deeper into her character.

Chris Wallace shows himself to be a chip off the old block in this area, saying that "it's great" when someone gets mad in an interview. "First of all, it's entertaining television. It makes news. It gets them off their talking points. They're revealing something about themselves and their character. My feeling is you don't want to let them roll over you, but let them vent. I mean, that's usually pretty entertaining." As an example, Wallace cites an interview he did for *Fox News Sunday* with Bill Clinton, in which the former president really blew his stack. "As you can imagine, working at Fox, it was hard to get him to agree to an interview," Wallace explains, but the former president came on to discuss the work of his charitable organization, the Clinton Global Initiative. A few minutes into the interview, Wallace asked Clinton why he hadn't done more to fight Al Qaeda and Osama bin Laden when he was president. "And he just went off," says Wallace. "I didn't even think this was an especially contentious question. I was shocked at his eruption and his anger. And his face turned all red, and he started wagging his finger, like the famous Monica Lewinsky sound bite, in my face." Wallace and Clinton then launched into a highly contentious discussion. "I worked hard to try to kill him," Clinton said of bin Laden. "I got closer to killing him than anybody has gotten since. And if I were still president, we'd have more than twenty thousand troops there trying to kill him." As the discussion got more and more heated, Wallace was thinking through how to play Clinton's eruption. "Finally, as he went on and on and how unfair Fox was, and 'We don't ask these kinds of questions of Republicans,' I spoke up." The interview made front-page news all over the country, which pleased Wallace. "I thought to myself, 'This is a hell of a news story I've got here. Nobody has ever seen Bill Clinton in public this way.'" But he's not expecting to land another interview with Clinton anytime soon.

What do you do if someone gets so angry that she walks out of an interview? Believe it or not, it's happened only rarely to the journalists we interviewed for this book and rarely to us, no matter how hard we've pushed the people we've interviewed. If it does happen, you just have to hope it's after you have already gotten the bulk of your interview done. "Burt Lancaster once walked out, because I was asking him about his temper. It was wonderful!" Mike remembers. "I remember distinctly standing side by side with him at the urinal before going into the studio, and I had read that he was quick to take offense. So as we were standing there side by side, I asked if there was anything that he prefer I not ask. He said, 'No, you can ask me anything.' So in the interview, I asked about his temper, and about the fact that he belted his seatmate on a transatlantic plane because he was not happy about something that had happened in the conversation." This sort of thing plays well on television, but it also burns bridges. Burt Lancaster, not surprisingly, never sat down with Mike again.

4

THE WORDS: CREATING GREAT REPORTING IN PRINT

Words have the power to both destroy and heal.
When words are both true and kind, they
can change our world.

—BUDDHIST PROVERB

Turning a pile of raw material into a polished report is probably the hardest part of journalism. It's certainly the most difficult to teach, because the rules can only take you so far; ultimately, every story is unique, and that means every story requires a unique approach.

That being said, behind each of those unique approaches lie some common basic principles and techniques that hold true for pretty much every story you'll tackle. If you begin each story you work on with an awareness of those ground rules, you'll have a good starting point for building your report. Those ground rules are what we'll be covering in this chapter and the next.

Standards to Meet

The ultimate goal of the story generation, research, and interviewing you do is to create a report that is meaningful and accurate. No matter what your medium, there are five overall standards you should meet in your report.

WERE YOU ACCURATE? Accuracy is the highest priority for any journalist. If what you write isn't accurate, you damage your own reputation and that of your organization. Accuracy begins with getting the basic facts right, of course, but it can mean a lot more than that as well. Did you frame the story correctly? Have you gotten the context for those facts right? Truly great reporters piece together information to build a picture of what they think happened, and then test the hypothesis they've constructed to make sure it's absolutely correct. Journalists can't be lazy or complacent or closed-minded if they want to be sure they're accurate. Accuracy takes work.

Double-checking facts has become fast and easy thanks to the Internet, as long as the sites you use to check information are accurate. (Generally, it's better to check information against a well-regarded publication or primary source rather than a user-curated site such as Wikipedia, which is known to be wrong at times.) Of course, computers have also made it easier for journalists to organize notes and document research. "I keep nearly all of my files electronically now," Kim Murphy of the *Los Angeles Times* writes. "All my notes are taken on the laptop (I drag it into all but the most inconvenient locales). I save e-mails, reports, news clips, info from websites, photos, even may scan relevant material from books. (That way, all of the documentation for a story can be stored in a single folder, and eventually burned onto a CD for long-term storage.)" She also starts a computer file for each story in which she logs the most important points, facts, ideas, and quotes, along with the source for each. "This file is an extremely invaluable aid to writing the story once I begin," explains Murphy. "I don't have to go searching for the numbers, dates, and places—it's all there."

HAVE YOU MADE IT RELEVANT? The facts you choose to report must be relevant to the story at hand, and relevant to the bulk of your audience. That's not always easy, especially when you're operating on a tight deadline. To keep reporting relevant, reporters must have a clear idea of their focus as they sort through the mountain of material they may have compiled. Before you write, it is usually helpful to formulate a six-word summary of what your story is really about, to help you sort out which parts of your reporting are most relevant. We'll talk more about this six-word technique in a moment.

HAVE YOU BEEN FAIR? As we discussed in Chapter 1, fairness means two things. First, your reporting has to be fair to the people you have used as sources. That means you must have quoted people correctly and accurately represented their views. Second, you must be fair in the way you present the story. That means your reporting has to be balanced and reflect all sides of the story. Eve Burton, the general counsel for the Hearst Corporation, notes that even-handed and balanced reporting isn't just ethical, it's also key to avoiding lawsuits. "If it's not something that's easily proven right or wrong, you always want to get both sides of the story," she says. "You'd be amazed at how many cases over the years I've defended where someone just didn't call the other side." She says reporters often use excuses to avoid the work of having to chase down the other side of the story—sometimes with disastrous results.

HAVE YOU BEEN LOGICAL? A good report, either print or broadcast, is driven by a logical progression linking one paragraph to the next. Without that progression, readers and viewers will get lost and lose the meaning of the report. We'll talk much more about specific techniques for organizing stories below, including the famous inverted pyramid, but we've found that the first step in creating a logical story lies in taking the time to properly organize your material before you actually sit down to write. Sort through all your material to determine what facts you know to be true. Write down the main points you want to make and the quotes you want to use. This not only makes the writing easier but also helps ensure that your best material gets into the story. "I write up a list—just a list—of all the important points I want to make in the story," explains Murphy, "things I want to make sure don't get left out, either 'on the other hands' or particularly good quotes or a scene that I know will fit somewhere, I just don't know where when I start." You never want to read a story and then realize you left out your juiciest quote . . . or a key fact.

Once you have your points and quotes laid out, start to think carefully about how best to present them. Every journalist has his or her own method for doing this, but we suggest you start by making a detailed, point-by-point outline for your story that lays out how each paragraph will read. Then check your logic. If you knew little about the story, would the outline be clear? Are the basic facts up front? Are characters introduced properly? Is the context being made clear? Then go through the same process again with the finished product, making sure you've ordered the facts in a way that a typical reader will be able to follow.

DID YOU USE THE RIGHT LANGUAGE? To be a good journalist, no matter what your medium, you must train yourself to be a wordsmith. That doesn't mean you should be writing fancy, flowery prose. It means being *precise.* One word, just one word, has the power to turn good writing into great writing, if that one word is precisely the right word for the job. That means you must choose your language with the utmost care. Most people are not used to thinking through the exact meaning of the words they use, but that's what's required to be truly precise. Beth won her one and only Emmy Award for a story she produced with Richard Roth, a longtime correspondent for CBS News, who is the best wordsmith with whom Beth has ever worked. "When Richard writes a piece, he seems to go through the dictionary to pick the most perfect word for everything," she explains. "His adjectives are precise. His verbs provide the exact description. Every word in his script seems to have been chosen above all others in the English language." Luckily, new tools such as online thesauruses and phrase finders make it much easier for people who are not great writers to find the right words.

WORKING UNDER DEADLINE. Some reporters thrive on deadlines; others hate the pressure of being forced to write. But given the twenty-four-hour news cycle and the constant need to stream fresh stories onto the Internet, there is more pressure on reporters than ever before to turn out lots of stories fast. The trick here, of course, lies in learning how to write fast without compromising accuracy or balance. "I do not include material in hastily written stories that I am not 100 percent sure of, even if it would be very nice to have that angle," explains Kim Murphy. "I do not put in one side and not the other. If I don't have time to call the other side (or they didn't call me back in time), I look for stuff they have said in the past that might help explain that there is another side to this story, and this is what they might have said had they had an opportunity."

It used to be that newspaper journalists had to file stories just once a day. Now, the papers' websites need frequent updates, even if the actual newspaper comes out only once a day. And that makes being accurate when under tight deadlines more important than ever. "In today's news environment, when you are facing constant deadlines on the Web, for blogs, et cetera, this is one of the biggest challenges reporters face," Murphy says. "But it's simply too awful to be wrong to take chances."

So here are a few tips for writing under deadline, applicable to all forms of media writing:

First, write a "minimum" story. Cover the most basic facts—who, what, where, when, why, and how, plus "so what?" and "what's next?"

Then go for a "maximum" story in the time you have left. Add in more details, put in additional quotes, and polish the writing.

Force yourself to write, even if you're not particularly happy with what you are producing. Once you've gotten something on paper, you can edit and improve what you have.

Use your time wisely. Make a plan of action, and force yourself to move on to the next part of your story even if you're not pleased with what you have down.

It's usually better to produce a mediocre report than to miss a deadline. It's hard to let go of something before you've got it just right, but deadlines and perfectionism don't mix. If you have the basic facts down correctly, it's almost always better to submit something rather than nothing. Editors hate to have to scramble for material at the last minute, and any publication would rather run a hastily written account of some hot piece of news than miss the story entirely.

It's all storytelling, you know.
That's what journalism is all about.
—TOM BROKAW, journalist and author

Choosing a Focus

We mentioned earlier that every story, whether for print or broadcast, usually starts with an outline, even if it's just a mental one. Outlining helps make your report logical, yes, but it can also be tremendously helpful in helping you choose a *focus* for your story.

Sometimes a story is so short or straightforward that there's really no question as to the focus. But often, when a story is longer or more complicated, there may be various ways to shape it. When Mike interviewed President Vladimir Putin of Russia in 2005, for instance, there could have been any number of ways to focus the story—on Putin's accomplishments, on his failures, on his relations with the United States. Mike felt that so much had already been written about all those things that he chose to focus on who Putin was as a person, and he engaged Putin with pictures of him and his family to get him talking. Choosing a focus is usually hardest when there are many different possibilities.

We are very fond of a method developed by Poynter Institute writing instructor Chip Scanlan, who suggests asking five questions to help focus a story. We include the method here with his permission:

What's the news? Tell your audience what is new and most important.

What's the story? This is *not* the same as "What's the news?" The news is the event itself; the story is the angle you're going to be taking in your report. What's the story you're choosing to tell here?

What's the image? That means the most memorable image in a photo or video about this story.

How can I tell it in six words? Boiling a story down to just six words is a great tool to help you choose the focus. It's difficult, but it works.

So what? As we said in Chapter 2, explaining why your audience should care also helps you get the focus right.

To see how this method works, imagine that you're covering a fire in your local post office. Officials caught the fire early, so no one was injured—but ten giant bins of mail were destroyed. You've interviewed people and watched the firefighters work. Now you have to focus the story before you sit down to write. And here's how you might use Scanlan's method to help you:

What's the news? A fire caused heavy damage to the local post office, but no one was hurt.

What's the story? Local residents have lost thousands of pieces of their mail.

What's the image? Postal workers carrying out boxes of half-burned letters dripping with the water used to extinguish the fire.

How can I tell it in six words or less? Postal fire causes local mail chaos.

So what? Thousands of local residents will have to try to sort out what was lost in the fire.

Now you can move on to cover the who, what, where, when, why, how, and what's next to create a story focused not only on the fire itself but also on the effects of the blaze on the local community. Clearly, if the fire had been fatal, or if the entire post office had burned to the ground, the focus of the story would have been different. Almost every story has more than one possible focus, and a hundred different reporters could cover the same story and produce a hundred different reports. That's one of the things that makes journalism so interesting.

Another tool that journalists sometimes use to focus their stories is to imagine that they are telling the story to another person—a mother or father, wife or husband, friend or colleague. Beth often advises her students to explain their story to a roommate before sitting down at the computer. Every person has a natural way of telling stories, and if you can tap in to your gut instincts for storytelling, you'll probably find it helpful.

Always grab the reader by the throat in the first paragraph,
sink your thumbs into his windpipe in the second,
and hold him against the wall until the tag line.

—PAUL O'NEIL, author

The Basics of Writing Hard News

We're now going to speak specifically to writing for print, starting with how to write a basic news story. The classic form for a hard news story is called the *inverted pyramid.* In an inverted pyramid, you arrange the information from most important to least important. Imagine an upside-down triangle with the most important fact first, the second most important fact second, and so on, and you'll understand why this form was given its name. Note that this structure means that facts will not necessarily be told in chronological order. The inverted pyramid requires that reporters judge what their readers need to know, then order the facts and work in enough background so that readers can understand what's going on. An inverted pyramid story also has to flow logically from start to finish.

This style of writing is used in newspapers, newsmagazines, wire services, and hard news Internet stories. It's applicable to any form of journalism where something's happening—news, sports, entertainment, or business. It's been used by generations of journalists to record world events.

Ron Blum, who covers sports for the Associated Press, uses the inverted pyramid in most breaking news stories, adjusting the content of his inverted pyramid each time he updates the story with fresh information. "The most important facts go in initial versions, which are designed for multiple media: broadcast, Internet, and print," he explains. "Later versions, especially those designed for newspapers, are written with more perspective and detail, sometimes looking ahead." New information may go at the top of the inverted pyramid or somewhere in the middle, depending on how it changes the story.

The inverted pyramid saves readers time, because they can get to the point of a story right away. It also makes life easy for editors, because if an article is too long to fit in the available space, they can just chop off the end and be sure they're omitting the least important facts. And the inverted pyramid is well suited to the way most people read news on computers nowadays. People today don't always read down through a whole story—they may read just the first couple of screens' worth of information. That makes it more important than ever that the beginning contain the key facts, which is just how the inverted pyramid works.

Every story—hard news or otherwise—begins with what's called the *lede*. (You may see this also spelled as *lead*.) The lede is the first sentence or two of a written or broadcast story. In a hard news story, the lede tells the most important thing or things that happened. To determine what goes in that first paragraph, you have to go back to that section we just had on focus. Ask yourself, "So what? Why should I care?" Let's say you're writing about a holdup in a store. Was it one of a spree? Was someone killed? Was Brad Pitt the victim? All those would affect what goes into the lede.

We'll talk more about crafting compelling ledes later in this chapter, but for now the most important things to remember about ledes are that they need to convey the essence of the news, and they have to catch your readers' attention. Imagine it this way: if a blaze broke out in your home, you wouldn't call the fire department and say, "Well, I was sitting in my house watching television, and then I smelled something, and then I decided that maybe the smell was getting worse, and then . . ." You would just yell, "*Fire!*" The lede of a hard-news, inverted-pyramid article is just like that. You get right to the point and grab people's attention.

Your whole inverted pyramid story has to cover all the basic questions of journalism—the five Ws and an H (who, what, where, when, why, and how), plus so what and what's next. You obviously can't fit all that information into the lede, but you have to put enough information in so that people will know what the story is really all about. So ask yourself what's absolutely crucial to the story. If someone read only one sentence of your story, what would you want him to know? Maybe your lede has the who, what, and why. Or maybe it's what, when, and how. It depends on the story.

BUILDING THE STORY. The next step after the lede is to build the top half of the article in a way that continues to present the most relevant information and keeps the interest of your readers. After all, news consumers now are so bombarded by information that reporters often have to fight to keep their attention. The key is to make sure you get the most important information near the beginning. "I read through my notes at least twice, sometimes three times, the first time to correct mistakes and subsequent times to find the five best things," says longtime print reporter Anthony Ramirez. "I make sure those five best things are mentioned or alluded to in the first ten percent of the story." Remember that idea of the "five best things." We'll come back to that again in the next chapter, when we discuss broadcasting.

Another helpful method for building a news article comes from Neil Hopp, a former newspaper reporter and editor who now oversees the student news publications at Central Michigan University. We share it here with his permission.

NEIL HOPP'S "FIRST FIVE" FORMULA

An effective lede. Focused, short, memorable.

A paragraph that **amplifies the lede.**

A paragraph that continues to **build detail.**

A nut graph, which presents the larger concept illustrated by the story, to provide context or tell reader why this story is important. (*Graph* is short for "paragraph." This is also sometimes spelled *graf*.)

A power quote. This is an interesting quote that propels meaning, not just a fluffy quote that fills space or gets in the way.

Hopp formalized the First Five when he took a job as the writing coach at a newspaper in the mid-1990s. "It's a commonsense approach to writing," Hopp says. "Whether a reporter is covering breaking news or employing storytelling techniques, this approach is a clear, concise method of starting a news story. It immediately communicates to the reader what the story is about, includes perspective and a 'voice' of an authoritative source. I've often instructed beginning reporters: 'You can't expect people to finish reading your stories if you don't hook them from the very beginning.'"

This method is a very malleable way to get into a story. If you use this formula, the lede obviously has to come first. But the other four elements can appear pretty much in any order. If you open a newspaper, you can usually find every variation possible of the First Five formula right there in print. You may see a lede, followed by a power quote, followed by more details about the lede. You may see a lede, followed by amplification, followed by a nut graph. There are different ways to play with the formula depending on the story, but the formula works.

There are plenty of other formulas out there, too, for building meaningful stories. The Gannett newspaper chain has one, for example, that says the first five paragraphs of a story have to cover four things: the news, the impact, the context, and the human dimension. That cuts things a different way but is clearly good advice.

THE DEVELOPMENT. Using the First Five will get you through a nice chunk of your story. But then what? That's when you have to go back to the idea of the inverted pyramid. You have to present the rest of the information from more important to less important. Make sure that one paragraph leads into the next. Think of it like putting together a puzzle: the pieces have to be lined up in the right way, and they have to click together. Remember that this is *not* an essay and *not* a paper for a class. A newspaper article should read like a newspaper article, with the news up top and details and background down below. Make sure you have included enough background so that a typical reader will be able to understand the meaning and context of your story. Then reread what you have written and try to judge whether someone who knows nothing about your story will be able to follow what you've written. It may help to imagine a real person you know reading the story. If you think your typical reader won't understand something, then add more detail or move around your paragraphs so they make better sense.

Last, imagine what would happen if your editor lopped off the last few paragraphs. Is there something in there that readers absolutely need to know? Then *move it up*—put it closer to the beginning of the story. If you're not sure you've gotten the order right, don't worry. That's why you have an editor. Then look for a logical place to stop the story, or for an appropriate quote on which to end. News stories often stop rather abruptly rather than ending gracefully.

Anthony Ramirez, who did his share of deadline reporting during nearly twenty years at the *New York Times*, adds three more excellent pieces of advice for finishing off a news story: "I remove adjectives and adverbs in my final copy and put them back only if they're essential. In a financial story or a story with numbers, I put a finger on the number in the document and then a finger on my story on the computer screen and make sure the numbers match. In any passage with negative connotations, I imagine my own name in place of the subject's."

It is hard news that catches readers. Features hold them.

—ALFRED HARMSWORTH, LORD NORTHCLIFFE,
newspaper publisher

Writing Feature Stories

A feature story is an article in a newspaper or magazine, or on a website that is meant not to report breaking news but rather to take an in-depth look at a subject. Features are often significantly longer than news articles, and unlike news stories, they don't always deal with ongoing events. Of course, there are so-called news features, which start with a piece of news and then expand upon it—not covering the news itself but exploring the effect of the news. But a feature can also be timeless. Open any women's or men's magazine, or the Sunday magazine inside your local newspaper, and what you are almost guaranteed to find is a feature story. Feature stories run the gamut in terms of subjects and style, and include profiles, reviews, investigations, and "service pieces," which offer helpful information on what to do or what to buy.

Features differ from news stories in some key ways. Unlike news stories, feature stories in print usually have characters in them who add a human touch and help sustain the interest of the reader. They usually take longer to report and write than news. And because they are longer and more in-depth than news stories, features give the writer more of a chance to use language and narrative creatively. They no longer use the inverted pyramid. Feature stories are organized more like a real story, with a beginning, some development, and an ending.

In a feature, you want to show people doing things. There is a voyeuristic quality to many good features, where the reporter allows you to feel like you were at the scene when things were happening. A long feature may have different scenes in which the action unfolds. In a news story, you may not have time to describe what's really going on in depth, but you often do in a feature story—and showing action is what gives features their power and texture.

Unlike in hard news stories, features should generally try to let the action and the dialogue, not the narration, carry the piece. The rule to follow in features is to show, not tell. "News stories don't have room for the long descriptive passages that are typical of novels. Still, few stories are not substantially improved by the little details, the few phrases of description, the narrative scene, that can bring them to cinematic life," explains Kim Murphy. Writers such as Murphy use action instead of narration wherever possible, describing in detail how someone does something, instead of just saying that she did it. The focus on action is what helps features keep moving along. Although features can be long, good organization and a focus on action will keep them from rambling or getting boring.

One reporter who incorporates action exceptionally well is Christopher Chivers, a correspondent for the *New York Times* who also contributes to the magazines *Esquire* and *Field and Stream*. A two-time Pulitzer Prize winner, Chivers came to journalism after serving as a U.S. Marine. That military training has given him a unique perspective that he incorporates into some of his best reporting. One of Chivers' specialities is spending time with U.S. soldiers in Iraq and Afghanistan, often in small outposts that are far from the main military bases. He'll spend weeks someplace, writing articles that show what daily life is like under fire. He doesn't say, "I spent today out on patrol with Zebra company"—he *shows* what happens to the troops, almost like a documentary filmmaker would. It makes for engrossing journalism. When Chivers goes out into the field, usually with photographer Tyler Hicks, he says he has one ambition: to show the lives of the soldiers as they are lived. "We typically arrange to stay for several weeks," Chivers explains. "We usually have little idea of what to expect, and we try simply to accompany the soldiers on their missions each day or night until the time is up. The stories always tell us what the stories are. We go in with an open mind, do the patrols, and listen. There is no real secret to it, beyond booking significant time and shedding any preconceived notions you may be carrying. That, and being in decent enough shape to work and walk alongside the soldiers."

How do you put together a feature story? Something like Neil Hopp's First Five rule doesn't really apply here, because you're not in a hurry to churn out all your information. Here's a more typical formula for writing a feature piece.

A STRUCTURE FOR FEATURES

An anecdotal lede. The lede often starts with a story about a person or people and a real-life experience that somehow relates to the topic of the story. The lede sets up a conflict or question, although it may not actually tell you what the story is really all about. The point of the anecdotal lede is simply to hook the reader.

A nut graph. Again, a nut graph is the paragraph that summarizes the essence of your story. It explains the larger trend you're explaining in your article. If you start with an anecdote, your reader may say, "Well, that's interesting. But what's the point? Why did you just tell me that story? What's the real issue at play here?" And that's what your nut graph explains.

Development of the story. Here's where you tell the main part of the story. There is often a chronological element to the storytelling, although there does not have to be. But the development is *not* in the inverted pyramid style of most important to least important.

Resolution. A feature story often ends up back where it begins. If you introduced characters at the beginning, you need to reveal what happened to them. If you asked a question, you must answer it. If you described a controversy, you must explain how it was resolved or why it has not yet been resolved.

This is a versatile formula, one that can be used for all kinds of features. If you don't believe us, look at pretty much any issue of the *Wall Street Journal*, which uses this construction over and over.

The formula works best when you start with a great story idea, researched well to make sure that you're not just writing the same article that dozens of other people have written already. If you're writing a story about how to apply eye makeup, for example, you're going to have to work extra hard to add something new and different. This is where having real people and strong characters in your article really helps to bring new light. And so does good reporting.

In features, it's crucial to interweave the action with the background, to help readers understand what's happened, what it means, and why it's important. "In general, longer stories tend to alternate between primary narrative elements (your main characters' stories) and background information (facts) conveying the bigger picture," says investigative reporter Michael Bronner. "A strong piece is one that finds the right rhythm as it moves back and forth between narrative and background elements." But you can't go too far afield. "Larding a story with facts or background information—or narrative, for that matter—that breaks this complementary rhythm can be counterproductive, as you're likely to distract or even lose your audience," he explains. It's a lot easier to put narration and background in separate, large blocks than to interweave them, but the reading experience is a lot more compelling when they're woven together.

To keep your feature focused, try to organize it into small pieces. Feature stories may be divided up into shorter units using subheadings to try to keep the story focused and well organized. Make sure one piece flows into the next. End with the resolution to the story. Explain what happened to the characters you introduced, or if there is no resolution, then explain why not or when resolution is expected. If you stick to the golden rule of "show, don't tell" whenever possible, you're likely to produce a feature that will interest your readers.

If you don't hit a newspaper reader between the eyes with your first sentence, there is no need of writing a second one.

—ARTHUR BRISBANE, newspaper editor

Writing Ledes with Style

It's worth taking an extra minute to focus on ledes, because writing good ledes is one of the most important skills a journalist can have. That holds true for broadcasting as well as print.

In fact, reporters tend to spend a disproportionate amount of their total writing time on the beginning of their stories, because a good opening makes the rest of the story flow more naturally. (The second hardest thing to write is the ending.) "Just as the longest journeys begin with the first step, it is crucial for me to get the lede right before I advance," explains Murphy. "In fact, I am unable to write a story that doesn't have a good beginning." A good opening needs to hook readers and get them to keep reading. A great lede will get someone to keep reading a story on a subject that may not really interest her very much. And a dry lede may deter a reader before the story's even gotten started.

Ledes can be memorable, fascinating, and engaging. Think of the greatest books of literature and you'll see some fantastic ledes. Think of the Bible: "In the beginning God created the heavens and the earth." Or take Charles Dickens' *A Tale of Two Cities*: "It was the best of times, it was the worst of times." Those are both novel and engrossing. You read those lines and want to hear what comes next. And that's the same feeling you want to invoke with a lede in journalism.

As we've discussed in this chapter, there are two types of ledes. The first is a hard news lede that gets right into the heart of the matter. This is also called a *direct lede*. The second kind is the type of lede you typically find on feature stories and is called an *indirect lede* or a *delayed lede*, because it doesn't immediately jump into the main point of the story. We used to call this a "feature lede" but don't anymore, because this kind of anecdotal lede appears more and more in hard news stories. Many newspapers are softening up the ledes on hard news stories to make it more likely that readers will read them.

Let's go back to that story about the fire at the post office. Here's how you can handle that story in two different ways.

> **Direct lede:** Thousands of pieces of mail were destroyed Monday in a fire that broke out in the Anysville central post office, causing chaos for hundreds of local residents who lost important documents.
>
> **Indirect lede:** Stacey Gordon, an Anysville teacher, is waiting for the paycheck she needs to make it through the month to arrive in the mail. But her wait may be fruitless, because thousands of pieces of mail were destroyed Monday in a fire at the central post office.

Direct ledes go straight into the action. They're the workhorse of journalism. Direct ledes usually contain specific information about what happened, when and where something occurred, and the source of the information. Attributing the information helps readers decide whether it's credible. Although these types of openings are fairly straightforward in terms of what they say, they can still be written with flair. Try to get in one strong verb or one carefully chosen adjective to add power to the writing—that's all you need to add pizzazz.

The indirect lede, even though it's now being used a lot in hard news, is most appropriate for features. You don't usually get many of the five Ws and an H in an indirect lede. You may get none of them at all. The point of the indirect lede is just to draw the reader in. When a feature starts with an indirect lede such as an anecdote, you may read the start of the story and not even know what it's really going to be about. But if the writer has piqued the reader's interest, then the lede is a success. Newsmagazines love the delayed lede. If you look at *Time*, *Newsweek*, and others, you'll see that many of their stories start out this way.

So how do you choose which lede style to use? Features should always get an indirect lede, but there are no absolute rules anymore when it comes to picking lede styles for hard news stories. "When there is breaking news, we go with hard news ledes. For sports game stories, especially big events, we have more features ledes," explains Ron Blum of AP. The wire service has even developed some creative ways to give its clients options when it comes to ledes. "Even with features ledes, we don't want to bury the news. Sometimes we craft ledes with a features first graph that could be lopped off if the end user wants to go with a harder lede in the second graph," Blum says. If you're not sure which one to pick, then talk it over with your editor. Some editors and some news organizations have a preference for one type of lede over another.

CRAFTING LEDES. So how do you craft a lede? It can be a real challenge to make your lede original and compelling. Reporters often play around with ideas for the lede in their heads as they do their reporting, trying to decide which kind of lede to use and looking for raw material that might make the lede interesting and fresh. A key to writing a good lede is keeping an open mind, according to the top editor of the *New York Times*. "Never get too locked in to what the story is," says Bill Keller. "You have to be open to the possibility that the story will go off in some completely unexpected direction. But that said, most reporters are writing the lede of their story in their head, and then rewriting it and reconceiving it all day long."

Journalists look for a logical starting point. "I have been often asked, but am unable to explain, how I figure out how to begin. It is simply a process of taking all the material now swirling in your brain and looking to see where a whirlpool develops. It simply happens," says Kim Murphy. She says that sometimes, when writing features, she may conceive of the nut graph first and then work backward. "You sort of know what your nut graph is going to be, and you have to arrive at a compelling way of getting there," she says.

When you're writing a direct lede, you usually start with the central idea. What happened? If you were telling a friend the story you're reporting, where would you start? Even though reporters rarely write the headlines for their stories, it may be helpful to imagine a possible headline for your story. Then try to use Chip Scanlan's idea and boil your story down to six words. That's usually the lede. But that can be hard to discern when you're sorting through a lot of news. Say you're covering a city council meeting where ten different things have been discussed. Deciding which of those belong in the lede is really tough, especially when you're a beginner. Sometimes reporters get around problems like that by using a *summary lede*, which explains that many things were discussed, and then talks about each in order of importance. Or sometimes they turn to senior colleagues or editors for help. But no matter what you decide to include, keep your direct lede short and try to add just one word to help it be memorable. Use two sentences if the first one gets too long.

Once you've figured out what you want to convey, you can work on expressing that idea with flair . . . but that requires hard work and creativity. Consider this lede from *Fortune*:

> Like a supermodel past her prime, Victoria's Secret is showing its age.

This lede is clever. It's not the classic "someone does something to someone" lede, which is why it's interesting. In this 2001 lede from the *Miami Herald*, the comparison makes it special:

> It took five months for the custody battle over Elian Gonzalez to build to a tense standoff. It took federal agents less than three minutes to end it.

Direct ledes such as this both cover the news and get readers interested by avoiding formulas and using language powerfully.

Writing a delayed lede gives you even more room for creativity. Consider this very original lede from the Pulitzer Prize–winning story "A Wicked Wind Takes Aim" by Julia Keller of the *Chicago Tribune*:

> Ten seconds. Count it: One. Two. Three. Four. Five. Six. Seven. Eight. Nine. Ten. Ten seconds was roughly how long it lasted. Nobody had a stopwatch, nothing can be proven definitively, but that's the consensus. The tornado that swooped through Utica at 6:09 p.m. April 20 took some 10

> seconds to do what it did. Ten seconds is barely a flicker. It's a long, deep breath. It's no time at all. It's an eternity.

Here you know basically that the story is going to be about a ten-second-long tornado, but not much more than that. Do you want to keep reading? We did.

More often, you start a feature story with an anecdotal lede. But you can't use just any anecdote—it's got to speak to the theme of the story, as in this Pulitzer-winning article, "New Approach to Lung Cancer: Being Aggressive" by Amy Dockser Marcus, one of a gripping *Wall Street Journal* series on people fighting cancer:

> In September 2001, at the age of 42, Lori Monroe was diagnosed with terminal lung cancer.
>
> The oncologist told her and her husband the cancer was inoperable, and the choice wasn't one treatment or another—but whether to do any treatment at all.
>
> Ms. Monroe, a nurse, was shocked. A month earlier, she had spent three weeks hiking in the mountains of Colorado. She had just returned from a trip water-skiing with her daughters, Emily and Alyson, who were 13 and 10 at the time. She felt and looked healthy. But her doctor said there was nothing Ms. Monroe could do.

Do you know what the story is going to be about? It will clearly involve people with inoperable cancer, but you don't really know if it will be about giving in or fighting back. The point of a lede like this is to get you interested in the story or the character. Do you want to know what happens to Lori Monroe? We sure did. And that's what an anecdotal lede is supposed to do—to get you hooked, so you keep reading.

Indirect ledes don't have to be long or complicated. Consider this lede, which Anthony Ramirez says is one of his favorites, written in August 2007 during a classic New York heat wave:

> At high noon yesterday, in the steamy subway station at Times Square, two sweating women were at dueling distance.

Do you know what's going to happen, or what the story's about? No. But do you want to keep reading? Yes! Or take another Ramirez lede, from 1987:

> Razor makers have always scratched their chins over what men want.

It's cute, it makes you smile, and it gets you interested in learning what men do want in their razors. It's not boring or ho-hum.

So the most important thing to do when writing an indirect lede is to choose your material carefully and with an open mind. And the more material you have to choose from, and the more potential characters you have met, the more likely it is that you will find a lede that will intrigue and interest your readers. Good reporting equals good ledes. Your language also really matters in a delayed lede. Pick descriptive words. You don't need to go for a word so unusual that people won't know what it means, or so graphic that people get disgusted, but you need to get people interested enough to keep reading.

Whenever you write, but particularly with indirect ledes, keep your writing clear. Stay away from the passive voice. The passive voice is bad because it can mask who is doing what to whom. Consider these two sentences: "The window had been forced open" is passive voice, but "Robbers forced the window open" is active voice. The combination of a subject, verb, and object is the clearest way to write in general, and definitely the best way to write for publication. And whichever type of lede you pick, it should never get too long. Some journalism textbooks say twenty-five words is enough for a lede, but we don't believe you can just pick a number like that. You have to ask yourself if someone can understand your lede and be intrigued by it, or if you have crammed in too much information. That is something you learn with experience, and with the help of a good editor.

To improve your command of language, it's well worth your time to look over the classic *The Elements of Style* by William Strunk Jr., revised by E. B. White. We think that book, originally written in the year that Mike was born—1918—is still the best guide to writing in the English language. It's loaded with useful advice for journalists, such as "Omit needless words." That's key for all writers, but especially journalists.

Sometimes journalists do what's called *burying the lede*. That means they omit a key piece of information from the lede, leaving the reader confused as to why the news is important. The big news has to go right at the top in a basic news story. You can't make people dig for it. For example, the Fordham school newspaper, the *Ram*, recently ran a very sad story about a student who had died during the summer right after her graduation. The story tried to be upbeat and focus on the wonderful life this young woman had led. But the writer had buried the lede. What was missing from the beginning of the article? The cause of death, which was more than halfway into the story. That's really burying the lede. When burying the lede happens, it's usually not that blatant. Often it happens when journalists write that a meeting happened or a speech was made, but not what was said. The lede should tell you the most important thing said or most important decision made, not just that the meeting or lecture happened. Consider, for example, a story that starts by saying your university has changed its stand on admissions policies and will put them into effect in two years. Again, that's burying the lede. What is the exact change the university made? *That's* the news.

There aren't any embarrassing questions—
just embarrassing answers.

—CARL T. ROWAN JR., journalist and diplomat

To Quote, or Not to Quote

Another key skill for journalists is learning how to handle quotations—what to quote, whom to quote, and when to quote. Quotes insert real people into your stories, enlivening and humanizing them. They add emotion and opinion to your reporting, as well as detail and drama. Another reason to use quotes is for *credibility.* As Kim Murphy explains, "Quotes not only make stories easier to believe—it's not just us saying something, it's someone who supposedly knows what he or she is talking about—but it also makes them more cinematic. Characters and voices bring a narrative to life and allow a story to be told not by us but by those who are making the news." In both broadcasting and print, great quotes make for great stories.

So what merits a direct quote? It is best to quote unique, strong, interesting material. Anything that will make your audience say, "Wow! That's new! I never heard that before" is worth a direct quote.

Letting the people in your stories talk is also an important way to establish their characters and to carry the action. "I like to let characters come to life as fully as possible in stories. To that end, I think it's critical to hear them speak," Michael Bronner says. "I like to use longer quotes, letting them breathe enough to hear the sound of the voice, the cadence of the thought, hesitation, anger, whatever. In that sense, I use quotes not to simply reiterate a point I've just made, but rather to convey information on multiple levels at once—from what they're saying to how they're saying it." Those kinds of quotes are particularly important in character-driven stories like features.

Reporters can also capture dialogue as they do their reporting and incorporate it into their stories, providing a way to hear the characters speak and see how they interact with each other. "I often think dialogue is more revealing and insightful than what we glean from interviews," says Christopher Chivers, who uses dialogue extensively in his features, especially those about American soldiers. "We need to do the interviews, of course. We need to be equipped with a broad base of knowledge, and specific knowledge for the story or beat we are working. But down at the lower levels, where the war is fought, the exchanges between soldiers can often be much richer (but not of course always) than what we hear when we ask questions." Bronner likes to quote not only dialogue but also other things that give insight into people, such as recordings or writings done by the interviewee. "I recently did a piece incorporating diary entries made secretly by an Iraqi prisoner in U.S. custody. They were fragmentary but raw, but particularly powerful for that," he says. Dialogue and quotes of other kinds of materials should be reserved for features, not hard news stories, where they can be given the space to play out well.

Perhaps more important than knowing when to quote is

knowing when *not* to quote. In general, it's best to paraphrase ordinary information that's not particularly new, interesting, or surprising. You should also paraphrase when people are a little long-winded, take a while to get to their point, or tell a story in a way that just doesn't contain good sound bites. Use only direct quotes that wow your audience.

To put it more succinctly, paraphrase facts, and then add quotes for color, emotion, and opinion. Reporters, as you may remember from Chapter 1, are not supposed to inject their own opinions into their stories. The reporter's voice is supposed to be balanced and objective. So a reporter's only way of injecting emotion and opinion into stories is by adding direct quotes containing the emotions and opinions of others.

You must be accurate when quoting. This sounds obvious, but you'd be surprised how many journalists get their quotes wrong. And there's really no excuse for inaccuracy. We recommend working with a tape or digital recorder. It helps ensure that you're accurate and lets you think about what people are saying instead of being a scribe. It also makes people stick to what they've said, which is why you may meet some resistance if you ask to record an interview. Argue that taping ensures accuracy and provides proof if someone claims to have been misquoted.

And, of course, you should never, ever make up a quote. It's the quickest way to end your career. We'll introduce you to some people who did so in Chapter 6—all of whom had to quit journalism.

Accuracy is about more than just getting the words right, though. If someone says something incorrect—makes a false claim, provides an incorrect piece of data—and you print it, you cannot protect yourself either morally or legally by saying,

"Well, I was only quoting what she said." You must verify everything you write, even if it's in the form of a quote from someone else. If you don't verify a piece of information that defames someone and it turns out to be wrong, you open yourself up to libel charges. If you're having trouble verifying something, you may need to question your source's motives. You need to make sure you're not being fed some wrong information in the hope that you'd print it.

To get the best quotes, speak with as many participants in a story as you can. You get better material when you get it straight from the horse's mouth, not second- or thirdhand. Cultivate many sources in many different areas. The broader your knowledge base, the deeper your knowledge. Remember to ask open-ended questions, to get your interview subjects to speak broadly. Really listen to people. That helps them relax, which helps them speak well. And never burn anyone by misquoting him or taking his words out of context. You don't ever want someone to accuse you of shoddy journalism.

SETTING UP QUOTES. Every time you use a quote in a story, you need to write an introductory sentence that sets up your quote. The sentence before a quotation should always present an idea that the quotation will confirm or explain. That lead-in sentence often works well when it is a paraphrase of something that person said. Consider the following examples.

Poor: *Gordon spoke about her missing check. "I really need the money, so I hope the check wasn't destroyed," she said.*

The lead-in here is poor because it doesn't add any real information. When you read the lead-in, you think, "Well, what did she say?"

Better: *Gordon said her check usually arrives on the 15th of the month. "I really need the money, so I hope the check wasn't destroyed," she said.*

The lead-in here is better because it does add some information, but it really does not present an idea that the quote will address.

Best: *Gordon said it will be hard to make it through the month if she doesn't get her check today. "I really need the money, so I hope the check wasn't destroyed," she said.*

This lead-in sentence is the best of the three, because it presents an idea that is confirmed by the direct quote.

To get the idea of writing lead-in sentences before quotes, think of how most students are taught to write papers. In an essay, you usually make a point, use a quote to back it up, and then explain who said the quote. It's the same way in journalism. You make an assertion in the lead-in to a quote, then confirm, add detail, or expound with the quote itself. We call this the *print triad*—assertion, quote, and attribution all have to work together. We'll get to a similar concept in broadcast writing in the next chapter.

Quotation is a serviceable substitute for wit.

—OSCAR WILDE, playwright and author

Understanding Attribution

When journalists speak about attribution, they actually mean two slightly different things: attributing information in their stories, and attributing the quotations that they use. Most of the information in your story needs to be attributed to either a person or a document. After all, people want to know where reporters got their information, so they can judge whether or not the information is reliable. You don't need to attribute anything that is generally known to most people, is a matter of public record, or is something that can be verified easily. But anything controversial, emotional, or opinionated needs attribution. Otherwise it will sound like the writer's opinion, and as we've said, journalists need to keep their own opinions out of their work. For example, you don't need to attribute the fact that Elvis Presley sold millions of records. That's a fact that's well known to most people. But you do need to attribute if you claim that Elvis is the greatest singer of all time, because that's up for debate. You should also provide the source of numbers such as statistics or poll data, to help your audience judge the authenticity of the information, because statistics can be bent to support a particular view. And you don't need to attribute facts if you're an eyewitness and have seen them happen. For instance, if you covered a building fire and saw the building collapse, you can write about it firsthand. But if you weren't there to see it, you should attribute information about the collapse to its source.

When you use quotations or dialogue, you must attribute each thing said, to make it clear who is speaking. Always attribute direct quotes, unless it would endanger the person or you've agreed to give someone anonymity. You generally attribute a quote at the end of the quotation's first sentence. If the direct quote is more than one sentence long, put the attribution after the first sentence. That's because the threesome of the lead-in sentence, the direct quote, and its attribution work well together. You make a point in the lead-in. Your reader then thinks, "Oh, yeah? Prove it!" Then you give the quote, which acts like proof. Then the reader thinks, "Oh, yeah? Says who?" And then you attribute the quotation. That troika of lead-in, quote, and attribution should appear together every time you use a quote, with the attribution in the correct place:

This is the perfect way to attribute a multiline quote:

> "Our mail service has always been great," Gordon said. "This fire has taken us all by surprise."

Use just one attribution, even if it's a multisentence quote. You don't need two, as here:

> "Our mail service has always been great," Gordon said. "This fire has taken us all by surprise," she added.

Don't attribute at the end of a multisentence quote, as here:

> "Our mail service has always been great. This fire has taken us all by surprise. We can hardly believe we've lost thousands of letters," Gordon said.

That's because as soon as there's a quote, your readers want to know who's speaking.

Attribution at the beginning does not work well:

> Gordon said, "Our mail service has always been great. This fire has taken us all by surprise."

It's just not very elegant, and gets in the way of the lead-in.

The first time you attribute a quote, identify the speaker

fully with name and title. On subsequent quotes, you'll have to follow the rules set by your publication. Some publications use courtesy titles such as *Mrs.* or *Dr.*, but others don't. But on second and subsequent references, omit your source's first name unless there's a concrete reason to use it—such as if you've interviewed two people with the same last name.

Two more small points about attribution. First, when you attribute a quotation, don't be afraid to overuse the word *said*. You can replace it, but many of the words you might use instead—words such as *claimed*, *maintained*, or *contended*—have subtle editorial overtones. *Said* is neutral, so it's often the best word to use. Second, when doing hard news reporting, don't try to read minds. If you're attributing people's opinions, do so based on what *they* say rather than on what *you* think. After all, you can't get inside another person's head to know what she is thinking. You don't know what someone else thinks, feels, believes, or desires. You only know what she says, so stick to that. It's okay to write "Megan Fox says *Transformers* is the greatest movie ever made" if she told you so in an interview. But you'd best not write "Megan Fox feels that *Transformers* is the greatest movie ever made," because that doesn't tell your audience how you know that to be the case. One of Beth's colleagues at Fordham, former *Wall Street Journal* reporter Arthur Hayes, hates the word *feels* so much that he has been known to actually fail students on an assignment if they write that someone they interviewed "feels" some way.

That said, when reporters do features, they often write about the thoughts and feelings of their main characters. For instance, Christopher Chivers' prize-winning piece for *Esquire* about the Beslan school siege contained long passages about what was going on in the minds of the terrorists and victims. Of course, he couldn't have known exactly what was going on in people's minds, but he tried to re-create his main characters' internal monologues accurately, based on dozens of interviews. Using some creative license is fine with features, as long as you know that the information you're putting into someone's mind is basically correct, but not with hard news.

ANONYMOUS SOURCES. Anonymous sources are a double-edged sword and need to be handled with great care. On one hand, they often give you the best information, because people feel freer to speak if they know that what they say won't be traceable to them. The famous example of this, of course, is Woodward and Bernstein's source Deep Throat, who broke the Watergate scandal and brought down a president. But anonymous sources can also pass you false information under the cloak of anonymity, which can damage your reputation. So if someone refuses to speak to you *on the record*—and you cannot print the information with his name and title—be sure to question his motives. "There are sources who are motivated by the desire to tell you something truthful and critical, and equally so by a desire for privacy," explains Michael Bronner. "It all comes down to the discipline of, first and foremost, constantly and rigorously evaluating why someone is telling you something. If you thoroughly fact-check and verify, which you have to do anyway, using a name becomes less important. You can tell when someone has an agenda, and that needs to be evaluated whether they're going on the record or not." Bronner says he becomes especially vigilant when anonymous information seems too good to be true. It often is.

It's crucial that reporters know their news organization's rules for giving anonymity and identifying sources, as they vary quite a lot. Most news organizations try to limit their reliance on nameless sources. "We are heavily discouraged from using anonymous sources, and use them only in the rare cases when information they transmit is so important it must be published, and to attribute it would cause harm to the source of the information, whether physical (might be arrested by the government or attacked by others) or perhaps loss of a job," explains Kim Murphy. "We are required to explain in the story why we agreed to use the material anonymously. This does absolutely nothing to lessen our standards for verification. We must be pretty darned sure the person is in a position to know what he's talking about, and is telling us the truth." Without a name, readers can have a hard time deciding how credible a piece of information is. And a news organization can also lose credibility if something attributed to an anonymous source turns out to be false. Then readers may think that the publication just made it up.

That's why many news organizations have very strict rules for attribution, especially when anonymity is involved. At CBS News, you usually need two independent sources to tell you something before you can report it. But you may be required to have three or more if they are anonymous sources, especially if the information is controversial.

If you decide to use an anonymous source, then absolutely run it by your editor first. And make absolutely sure to clarify the rules for attribution with your source. There are slightly different terms for *anonymity*, and it is crucial that the reporter and source agree on the definitions. People often get them wrong. *On background* usually means that information can be used without a source's name and title, but with some reference to the speaker's background—like "an official at the Justice Department said." *On deep background* means a journalist cannot use a source's name or any other information that might cause him or her to be identifiable—like "one official said." *Off the record* usually means that the reporter cannot print the information at all—that it's just for the reporter's own knowledge. Then why is it valuable? Because other sources might be able to confirm it, and they might not insist that the information stay off the record. If someone tells you something off the record, get in the habit of asking if the source might give you a document that backs up what he or she says, and of asking the source to recommend someone who might confirm the information.

5

THE SOUND AND THE PICTURES: CREATING GREAT REPORTING FOR BROADCAST OR INTERNET

Try to be conspicuously accurate in everything, pictures as well as text. Truth is not only stranger than fiction, it is more interesting.

—WILLIAM RANDOLPH HEARST, newspaper magnate

Going from print into broadcasting strikes us as like going from driving to flying—the basic idea is the same, but you have additional dimensions to consider. Broadcasting differs from print in some key ways. First, in broadcasting, you get only one chance to make yourself understood. People can't easily go back and watch or listen again (despite website videos and YouTube), so you have to make yourself crystal clear the first time around, while with print, people can always go back and reread a sentence they don't understand. In broadcasting, you're telling a story, and the structure you use has to reflect that. Radio and television stories have a beginning, middle, and end—even if they're just fifteen seconds long. They're also inherently personal. Even though a report may reach millions of people, a broadcaster speaks to just one person at a time. In other words, the reporter up on the screen or on the radio seems to be speaking directly to you, the listener. In the best cases, reporters and anchors are able to create a personal connection with members of the audience, which helps viewers stay interested. But most of all, broadcasting allows journalists to use sound and pictures in telling their stories. Those are powerful tools, and we'll spend much of this chapter explaining how to make words, sounds, and pictures work together.

We also discuss writing for the Internet in this chapter. We should note that we do *not* mean to understate the Internet's importance to the news business by devoting only part of a chapter to it; we realize that it's only a matter of time before the Internet is the main news source for everyone (in fact, polls show that it's already the main source for people under thirty, and second only to television for those over thirty). But as we'll demonstrate later in this chapter, if you absorb the basics of print and broadcast reporting taught in these pages, you'll be well prepared to do solid Internet reporting as well.

The Essentials of Broadcasting

The essence of broadcasting is really very simple. In television, the pictures have to tell the story. In radio, the sound has to tell the story. That means that if you turn off the sound of your television and just watch the video, or if you were to just hear the sounds used in a radio piece without any narration, you should still know what's going on. Beth produced a taped TV report (called a *package*) not long after joining CBS News that illustrates this concept perfectly, about how St. Basil's Cathedral—the magnificent onion-domed church on Red Square in Moscow—had fallen into disrepair. Correspondent

Richard Threlkeld wrote a beautiful script, but viewers really didn't need his words because they could simply *see* the story. The video showed the church's walls covered with graffiti, the frescos faded, and the stairways literally crumbling. When the pictures don't really tell the story, they're called *wallpaper*—and that's what you want to avoid.

Broadcast writing is conversational. You use only those words or phrases that you'd use in everyday conversation. "I lean back and I try to think, 'Okay, how would I tell this to my daughters and my husband, who are pretty smart, but might not be too interested in this story?'" says Lin Garlick, of CBS Newspath. "And generally speaking, it comes to me in Lin-speak, not fancy journalism-speak. And it's Lin-speak that should go on the page—very conversational, very matter-of-fact." The best broadcasters write the way they speak. "When I write, I read the words out loud to make sure it sounds natural," says Robert Smith, a New York–based correspondent for National Public Radio (NPR). "When we edit, the editor doesn't look at my script, but listens to me read and play it." Contractions are fine, because that's how people really talk. Brief, declarative sentences are best, because short sentences are easier to absorb. If you have more than two commas in your sentence, it's probably too long for broadcast.

As in print, you should try to use the active voice in your writing—but in broadcast, you also try to use the present tense. Your goal is to emphasize that this is all happening today, right now. In fact, broadcasting is increasingly about the here and now. There's more live news than ever, and the rise of cable news has given the news business a new immediacy. That means broadcasters tend to use the present tense whenever possible, even if they have to cheat a little to do it. A television station might report, "Passengers are recovering tonight from their harrowing plane crash in the Hudson River," not "The passengers made it off the plane that crashed into the Hudson River, and were moved to area hospitals." See the trick? The first sentence makes it seem that the action is still going on. That's typical of a broadcasting script.

Creating a broadcast report, particularly a television report, is really a team effort. You have producers to help make arrangements, camera people, sound engineers, anchors, correspondents, and editors all working together to create the story, plus engineers and program executives who execute and shape programming. The collaboration is what makes it fun, and when the team works well together, it's really a dream. "The greatest thing about *60 Minutes* is the people who work here, and all of them devote themselves to making me look better. I never forget that," says correspondent Scott Pelley. "I work with the greatest producers and reporters and cameramen and editors and management in all of news. So when you have that team—and this is a team sport we play, you know—the awards come, because the work can be extraordinary."

This also means that the process of creating broadcast reports is a lot more complicated than print. In broadcasting, a lot of the steps are interdependent, meaning you have to think about doing lots of things well at once. You can't just focus on the words alone, for example; rather, as you write, you have to consider simultaneously what the pictures or sound will be. The logistics in broadcasting are also way more complicated than print, requiring radio and television reporters to think about things such as gear and transmission options as well as the journalism. Beth remembers the first time she went on the road with her producer, Alexei Kuznetsov. He'd spent more than a decade as a reporter for the *Los Angeles Times* before joining CBS News, and was used to going on trips with a few reporter's notebooks and a little tape recorder. On his first CBS trip, Kuznetsov looked at the pile of about four hundred pounds of gear that the cameraman, David Grout, had laid out for the trip. There were lights, a tripod, camera batteries, chargers, extra lenses, tapes, a sound mixer, a microphone on an extendable pole, and a camera. Dismayed by the amount of equipment he would have to carry, Kuznetsov exclaimed, "Look at this stuff!" "Yeah," responded Grout proudly. "I was able to pack really light!"

It seems to go directly to one's brain.
There are no pictures to distract.
—BOB EDWARDS, journalist and author

The Joys of Radio

We haven't had the chance to say too much about radio so far, which is a medium we both adore. Mike started his career in radio, and Beth did some of her best work in radio news. So before we get any further into the study of broadcasting, we want to talk specifically about the wonders of radio, many of which seem to be lost on younger generations. "Friends my age joke that we can't have a conversation of more than five minutes without mentioning some radio report we heard. But young people are missing that," Beth laments. People tend to think that radio is useful because it's easy to do something else while you listen. It is, but it's also a delightful medium for journalism.

The best radio writers are able to create pictures with

words. Whether they are writing a twenty-second news brief or a ten-minute feature, good radio writers create imagery that transports listeners to the scene of the action. They also use sound—of both people and things—to add depth to their pieces. "Sound is everything in radio. Otherwise we're just reading newspapers on the air," explains NPR's Smith. "I think it's important to realize that sound to a radio reporter isn't just the background audio of a scene that we pump in under our scripts. A good radio reporter thinks in sounds throughout the whole process. We pick out stories that have great opportunities for audio. We plan out scenes based on what sounds are there." Hearing is believing. Saying that there's a big hurricane is one thing. Hearing the wind tear the roof off a building is entirely another.

So doing radio requires collecting sound—and that takes planning. "Beginners in radio will often just arrive at a place, listen for something happening, and hold up a mic. We call this generic sound *ambiance*, and sometimes it's great," explains Smith. "But I compare it to a photographer taking a picture of a crowd. You get an idea of the scale of something, but no details. No memorable information. Once you've been in radio a while you'll start to learn that sounds in a scene are layered. You'll want to get close-ups of some sounds, faraway recordings of others. You also learn that sounds change during a scene. What sounds begin an event? What sounds end it? You really are deconstructing a place into its audio pieces and reassembling it back in the studio." Smith says he usually carries around a digital audio recorder, along with two different microphones—one for general recording and one for faraway sounds. Recording sound digitally makes it easier to edit. You can feed the sound into a computer editing program and easily interweave it with narration into a whole report.

Radio reporters usually gather their own sound. Sometimes that's easy, but sometimes it requires them to be creative. "A lot of my research is about planning to be in the right place at the right time," Smith explains. "If it's something sound-rich, like a protest or performance or police action, then it's easy. Show up, get close, and keep recording. And if the action is quiet, then I need to find someone to describe it to me. Maybe it's a scientist narrating as he runs tests on a sample, or something like that." If a reporter is on the scene, he or she can also ask questions, to shape the material that will go into the report.

We cannot make good news out of bad practice.

—EDWARD R. MURROW, journalist

Planning for Success in Broadcasting

Doing a successful broadcast story consists of five steps: preparing and researching, recording your pictures and/or sound, reviewing your material, writing, and editing. We'll address each of these in order, starting with the initial preparation.

When you're doing a television or radio report, everything we taught you earlier in the book about planning your story still holds true. You still need to identify a good story and research it well before anything else can happen. But from the very beginning, you should be asking yourself whether the story will work for broadcast. What sound and pictures will you be able to get? You want more than just people talking. When a story is all talking heads, it can get boring. If you're doing a report for television, you want different kinds of pictures to use in your story. These are the images that you'll show when you don't show someone speaking. The better these shots are in telling your story, the better your story will turn out. We say that some stories are just "good picture stories," meaning that the pictures are full of action. Television loves action shots and hates static ones. This need for pictures also explains why television is not particularly good at doing stories about things that haven't yet happened. The lack of pictures means that visually, your "before" story is likely to be made up primarily of wallpaper.

Each place or person you shoot or record for your story is called an *element*. Let's say you're shooting a story about a medical breakthrough. Your elements might include a hospital where the new breakthrough is being used successfully, the laboratory where it was discovered, and interviews with doctors and patients. You always try to have enough elements to do a wide-ranging and educational story. "I like to have at least three separate sections in any piece, so it creates a sense of movement. Like we've accomplished something," says Smith. The longer your story, the more elements you need. Sometimes you'll end up not using an element, either because the shoot didn't work out as planned or because you can't fit it in, but because shooting an element is time-consuming and may have costs associated with it such as overtime or travel, broadcast professionals try to use what they shoot and shoot only what they need.

Never assume that you can just waltz in somewhere and shoot the elements you want. Professional audio and video recording usually requires advance permission if you'll be on private property. On public property it's much easier to shoot, and as long as you're accredited you usually don't have to ask for permission. But if you need to shoot in a factory, you can't just show up at the gate with your cameras and gear and expect to be let in—get permission first.

In fact, if there is one overarching mantra for doing television, it's "never assume." Assuming things often leads to disaster, as in "I thought you were bringing the camera," or "I assumed there would be electricity there," or "I assumed we could get in without a visa."

It's in this planning stage that broadcasters start to pick their characters. Television and radio reports are character-driven, much more so than print. Real people are what make broadcast stories interesting, especially when the main characters have had amazing experiences or are well spoken. So television and radio people spend time looking for the right characters to bring a story to life. When deciding whether or not to do a particular story, the existence of good characters is one of the deciding factors. "You just don't want to go ahead unless you think that the story is really going to work for you. And therefore you try to find the main character and a couple of other supporting characters before you ever commit to actually shooting the piece," explains Robert Anderson, Mike's longtime producer at *60 Minutes*. "We spend a lot of time researching stories that we don't do because either the premise doesn't hold up, the facts don't sustain the premise, or we can't find the characters through whom to tell it."

When you're looking for the characters for a broadcast story, the manner in which people speak is a factor in deciding who you might want to interview. If someone has a speech impediment or a very thick accent, or doesn't speak English well, that person may not play well on TV or radio. And television is a visual medium, so, unfortunately, the way a person looks may also come into play. If someone has a gross disfiguration, or something that will keep viewers from listening to what that person is saying, you may want to include someone else in your report.

You also now have to think about what sounds you'll want to include, whether you're doing radio or television. There are actually two categories of sound. First are the snippets of ambient sound you collect for your radio or television piece. This is called *natural sound*, although it doesn't have to occur naturally. A clock chiming or a car engine revving would still be called natural sound. "Natural" simply means that the sound is not from an interview. Recording this kind of sound often requires being proactive in a way you don't necessarily need to be when you work in print. "Sometimes you have to be pushy," says Smith. "When I profiled the men restoring the lion statues at the New York Public Library, I made them walk me through each step—the washing, the brushing, the blow-drying—so I could get each sound separately. Then I recorded them doing it all at once. Then I interviewed them with no sounds behind them. This allows me to relayer everything and more vividly re-create the scene than if I had just stood there with a microphone for an hour." Natural sounds are also used in television reports to add to the pictures and to break up the narration. If you pay careful to attention to most video reports, you'll notice moments when the narration stops for a bit of natural sound, giving the viewer a moment to absorb what he's just been told.

The second type of sound is the more obvious one—recordings of interviews. Sometimes you might play a whole interview on the air, but usually you extract the best pieces of an interview—the *sound bites*—and use only those in your reports. The criteria for choosing sound bites for broadcast is much the same as choosing direct quotes for print—you're looking for nuggets of emotion or opinion, things that can't be relayed by the reporter's narration. "I record a lot of back-and-forths between myself and the person," explains Smith. "I don't try to be a sterile reporter; you'll only get sterile responses back. Instead, I tell stories, I joke, I make assumptions and let the person correct me. I emote so they'll emote."

Of course, reporters don't always have the luxury of time to prepare this way. If you're doing a feature story, you'll probably have time to choose your elements carefully and make sure that you've picked the very best material to shoot or record. But if you're covering breaking news, you may not get to choose very much. Oftentimes covering breaking news is about doing the best you can with the pictures and sound you have or can get quickly and easily. In those situations, reporters often use sound and pictures that other people have gathered. Agencies such as Reuters Television and Associated Press Television News provide both radio and television broadcasters with material, so correspondents don't necessarily have to be where news is happening. Broadcasters would rather have their own coverage on-site, of course, but sometimes the news is happening so far away that their reporters can't get there in time, or the trip is so expensive that the news organization decides it's not worth the money to send someone there. Networks also often rely on their affiliated local stations for video and audio.

And, as when working on a short deadline in print, remember that *something* is usually better than nothing. With breaking news, perfection's often not achievable, and an editor or producer would much rather have a half-decent report to air than nothing at all.

The wonderful thing about television is the immediate impact of pictures of current events.

—WILL MCDONOUGH, sportswriter and columnist

Recording

Once you know what elements you want to focus on, you've got to capture them for broadcast. In television, this is generally the work of a cameraperson, but even if you're going to work as a producer or correspondent, you need to know the basics of camera work and terminology. Besides, if you're going to be a journalist nowadays, it's highly likely that you'll be asked to shoot video at some point in your career.

Television needs different kinds of shots to help fool the eye in editing. The cameraperson may do a *wide shot*, which shows a broad area such as a whole building or a crowd of people; a *medium shot*, which shows a person or two or perhaps a small group doing something; or a *close-up*, which shows a person's face or hands or other details. To understand what different shots are like, imagine that you've just walked into a new classroom for the first time. First, your eyes would probably take in the equivalent to a wide shot, which in this case would be the whole room. Then maybe you would focus on a person or two inside who you already know. That's a medium shot. Then you might focus on the professor's face as the lecture begins. That's a close-up. When doing a television piece, you may be asked to shoot a variety of generic shots of something happening or a place where you are filming. These shots, called *B-roll*, are used to help cover the narration in a television piece.

APPEARING ON CAMERA. The most familiar element of the television package is probably the *standup*. This is the "piece to camera" in which the correspondent talks right to the audience to add information or analysis. You've seen these countless times if you watch television news regularly. In feature stories, the standup's often inserted in the middle of the piece, where it's called a *standup bridge*. That's because it connects the first part of the piece to the second part. In breaking news stories, a standup's often at the end of a piece. Standups are always taped and rarely are put at the beginning of a report, although a reporter may start or end a piece by appearing live. More about that in a moment.

The standup is the reporter's opportunity for face time, and believe us, correspondents live or die by face time. But the standup also shows that the reporter is at the place where the action is happening, thereby increasing credibility, and it allows the viewer to connect with the reporter, increasing an audience member's interest in the story. Ideally, frequent viewers will come to recognize the reporters on a network and begin to trust them. A standup also allows a reporter to talk about something important for which there may or may not be video.

Some networks like static standups, where the reporter just stands there and talks. Others like to *push in* on the reporter, or zoom in closer—a technique that makes the words of the reporter seem even more important. But standups in which the reporter walks or shows something are common, too, especially in local news. The tone and the pace of the standup ideally should match the tone and pace of the *track*—the narration. To record the narration is also called *to track*. It all needs to sound conversational to work.

Reporters often open or close their reports with a live shot, which may be done instead of a standup or in addition to it. Live opens and closes usually feature the reporter at the scene of the story, giving the latest developments. This format has gotten more and more popular over the years, as the technology to broadcast live news has improved and gotten cheaper. For local news in particular, stations like to emphasize that they're there live, on the scene of a breaking story. When going live, the reporter may simply speak with the anchor, or may segue into a taped report, called an *insert*. A typical James Ford piece on WPIX looks like this: the anchor introduces him, then Ford reports live from the scene of the news, then the station plays his insert—the short taped report Ford has narrated—then he returns live to close out the report.

When doing live shots, reporters speak in a way that tries to establish their credibility. "I always talk like I'm communicating with one person, and try as often as possible to use the fact that I have a live picture behind me to state the relevance and timeliness of a story," Ford says. To illustrate, he cites an introduction he used for a story that updated the status of a police officer who got shot: "The police officer who was shot is here on the fourth floor in the intensive care unit, and the faces of his family and friends we've seen come and go show just how emotional a day it's been for them." His comments emphasize that he's at the scene, so he knows what he's talking about.

SETUPS AND CUTAWAYS. Something else you'll need to know about is the *setup shot*. These are the pictures that will roll to introduce people you interviewed, before they give a quotation. The text might say something like, "John Brown, a professor of politics at Northwestern University, says that reforming health care is the president's biggest challenge." So you need to see Professor John Brown there doing something before you hear what he has to say. There are two classic setup shots. The first is the person walking, either alone or with the correspondent. Just make sure the people leave the frame at the end of the shot, for editing purposes—meaning that they should seem to walk completely out of the picture. The second classic setup shot is the work shot. If it's someone in an office, you usually get the interviewee on the phone or on the computer. But a setup shot can be anything the person might naturally be doing. A baker might be baking, a chef cooking, a carpenter hammering, and so on. You also want a close-up shot to use in editing, like someone's fingers on a keyboard. Beth learned about the importance of setup shots the hard way. She filmed her first TV interview with an art dealer in Moscow and thought it all went well until her boss asked to see the setup shot. Beth didn't have one, so there was no material to use in editing the piece. She had to call this art dealer to ask him to come in the next day wearing the same clothes he had worn for the interview, to do setup shots. It was pretty embarrassing.

Another kind of shot you should know about is the *cutaway*. This is a shot that cuts away from the action to show something else, typically either a shot of the reporter listening, a close-up of someone's hands as he or she is talking, or the audience if there's a speech. This shot is crucial to editing, because it allows you to remove material and edit the parts back together seamlessly. In particular, cutaways are used all the time to meld two sound bites together. To understand how this is done, remember that you can record audio and video separately when you're editing your piece. Let's say someone said something great, then said something you don't need, and then said a second thing you'd like to use. To remove what you don't need, start by showing the audio and video of the first sound bite. Then cut to video of a cutaway, such as the reporter listening, as you begin the audio of the second sound bite. Then cut back to the video of the second sound bite as its audio continues. When done right, it should appear to be one single, seamless sound bite, with a shot of the reporter listening in the middle. Just remember that reporters should not be nodding in a cutaway as someone talks. That would imply that the reporter approves of what the interviewee is saying, which is a breach of the code of objectivity. A stationary listening shot or a neutral head movement works best.

On the technical side, lighting can make or break your shoot. Either too dark or too bright and your video is unusable. And the quality of the sound matters, too, both for television and for radio. An interview done in a noisy location might not be audible. One good term to know is *white balance*, which is a kind of light measurement. The cameraperson must focus the camera on a sheet of white paper, or something else that is pure white, every time he or she shoots in a new locale. You'll impress your coworkers by whipping out a piece of white printer paper when it's time for a balance.

Another mantra of television is "You're only as good as your gear." Nearly every television journalist has a story about equipment that wouldn't work, causing a catastrophe. Beth remembers landing an interview with a Bolshoi Theater ballerina whose male partners were complaining that she was too heavy to lift. "Our bosses loved the 'fat ballerina' story, and were delighted that she sat down to talk with us," Beth remembers. "Except something went wrong inside a sound cable, so there was some clicking that we didn't hear when we were taping. Most of the interview was unusable." You can't always catch technical problems like that, but knowing the basic functions of gear such as cameras, sound mixers, and lights increases your value to your team.

When television is good, nothing is better.
When it's bad, nothing is worse.

—NEWTON N. MINOW, former chair,
Federal Communications Commission

Culling Your Material

Now that your video is shot, your sound recorded, and all your interviews done, you need to organize the story and pick out the best material. Then, when you write, you will choose the words to make the most of the pictures or sound you choose.

Which are your best pictures? They're usually the ones that help tell the story. Some shots have key actions. Some are close-ups. Some are vistas. Some are simply beautiful pictures, like paintings, which we call *beauty shots*. These pictures have to be well shot—nothing blurry or poorly lit—and well composed.

And what about the sound? Good sound means both high-quality natural sound and the best sound bites. In terms of natural sound, you'll be looking for sounds with power—sirens, wind, the sizzle of meat on a grill, the crack of a baseball bat. And in terms of sound bites, you'll be searching for the wittiest, smartest, funniest, most surprising, most important, or most succinct things people said. Just as in print, make every quote count. "I try to pick out interview excerpts that have more than just information," says Robert Smith of NPR. "I can sum up facts and figures. I want quotes that show passion, reflection, engagement, humor, or some other emotion." He'll even play sounds for interview subjects and get them to comment, which is a nice way to employ both varieties of sound.

The first step in culling material is to go through and log everything you've gathered—meaning to create detailed notes about the best pictures and sound. Working in broadcast means lots of logging tape—or, nowadays, logging disks and computer files. If you're on deadline, you may do your logs very quickly, looking for a few key sound bites and pictures. But if you're working on a long-form piece or have no tight deadline, you may do very detailed and elaborate logs. When you log, you describe the audio and video in detail, noting not just content but information such as time codes and whether something is shot wide, medium, or in close-up. Logs also help reporters identify potential sound bites by summarizing or completely transcribing interviews, allowing people to find material quickly and easily. At *60 Minutes*, all interviews are transcribed completely, but most reporters elsewhere don't have the time or money to do that. Most broadcasters we know transcribe only the parts of interviews that might actually make it into the final report, and summarize the rest.

By this phase of the process, you should have a clear perception of your story. Remember that TV and radio stories are all about boiling down complex ideas to their essence. Viewers want to know pretty quickly why a story is important, or they tend to tune out. And besides, most television and Web video stories are pretty short, meaning there's not always a lot of time to play around. If you're not sure you know what your story is, now is the time to clarify it in your mind. Remember our focus exercises from the last chapter? Boil your story down to just a few words. "I learned an excellent lesson from the Poynter Institute when I did a fellowship there years ago, and I never forgot it: if you can't write a story *in three words*, you're not focused enough on the nub of the story," notes James Ford of WPIX-TV. "So before I write my full script, I write the story out in three words first. So my story on divers, recovery crews, and investigators salvaging aircraft wreckage as they try to figure out what caused a fatal crash over the Hudson River started out as 'Aircrash Recovery Challenges.' I wrote the track, and picked video and sound from there." You'll find it very hard to write a compelling story if you haven't first clarified in your mind what you want to say.

Reporters may write an outline at this point in the process, with ideas for the narration and quotations. The outline will focus on the flow of the story, to help keep things clear. The outline notes how to present the story in a super-organized way, from A to B to C, and then to D. This is obviously a lot easier to do in a short piece than in a long one—which is why a journalist may cut a long broadcast piece into episodes, to make it easier to organize. If you're doing a really long piece, such as an hourlong show, the commercial breaks actually force you to think in episodes.

We usually start our outlines by identifying the best quotes and then putting them into an order that makes sense. We do this by imagining how we'd tell the story to a typical viewer who's intelligent but may not know much about what we're reporting. When choosing quotes, remember that you can convey any needed facts in your narration, but, as in a print piece, you need the people you interview to inject the opinion and emotion. Next we try to outline what we'd need to say in the lines of narration that precede and follow the quotes. Then we try to come up with a lede that will hook the audience, and an ending that adds a conclusion without injecting opinion. When the outline is done, it forms a skeleton on which we can hang the rest of the story.

Creativity is piercing the mundane to find the marvelous.

—BILL MOYERS, journalist and author

Writing for Broadcast

Once you have a decent outline and know your best pictures, sounds, and quotes, you're ready to start writing. Virtually all of the general rules for writing for broadcast apply to both radio and television, and they all flow from a single principle: in TV and radio, your goal is to let the pictures and sounds do as much of the work as possible. The pictures and sounds provide what the narration doesn't.

That means there's really no room for flowery writing, extra details, or long-winded discussions. Use your words economically. Don't use a whole sentence when one phrase can do. Don't use a phrase when a word will do. Look at every single word you've written and ask yourself if you really need it. Condense every sentence to the fewest possible total words. Keep your sentences short and usually in the present tense. Less is more. In fact, the whole text of a typical two-minute broadcast story is just a few paragraphs long.

Knowing that, you might think that newspapers are a superior form of communication, because they contain so much more detail. But then think about big events such as 9/11, Hurricane Katrina, or the election of our first African American president, and you'll realize that broadcasting has a different kind of power than print.

When you're ready to write, you have to keep your pictures and sound in mind as you're composing the words. In television, you must have a conception of what video you will be showing alongside every phrase, so that the words will complement the pictures, not repeat them. "The pictures drive the narrative," says James Ford of WPIX-TV. "When I write, if I have in mind the video available to me, I can better drive home my information, and match that information with pictures in the final edit." Never tell viewers what they can already see or hear. Use the words to tell them what they *cannot* see or hear. Write to the edge of the pictures with your narration, like this:

Example 1: Video of a protest against teacher layoffs going on in a driving rain.

Poor: *"Protesters gathered in the rain to protest teacher layoffs."* It repeats what you're seeing, and doesn't add much additional information.

Better: *"Not even a driving rain could keep these people from protesting the city's decision to lay off fifty teachers."* Plays off the rain, adds additional material, but still tells you what you already see.

Best: *"They gathered in dismal weather to protest what they're calling a dismal decision—the layoff of fifty city teachers."* The text doesn't repeat what you can see, adds some clever writing, and also contains details.

Example 2: Video of Mayor Joe Wilson, who's running for reelection, coming out of voting booth.

Poor: *"Mayor Wilson, who's up for reelection, voted this morning."* It repeats what you're seeing, and doesn't add much information.

Better: *"At Ward Elementary School, Mayor Wilson cast his ballot this morning, in what's seen as a tight race."* It adds some new information, and explains what you see.

Best: *"The Mayor may be smiling—but his reelection race* *is too close to call."* Plays off of and goes beyond the pictures; tries to add clever writing.

Example 3: After a fire at the post office, firefighters push out rolling bins of wet mail.

Poor: *"Thousands of pieces of mail were drenched when firefighters extinguished the fire at the central post office."* This line mostly repeats what you see.

Better: *"It took firefighters two hours to bring the blaze under control, drenching most of the building and its contents."* This is better because it adds details you can't see, but also tells you something you can see.

Best: *"The loss of this much mail will cause havoc for some local residents."* Best because it references the pictures, is factual, and goes beyond what you can see.

Try to train yourself to take one step away from the pictures and augment them rather than describe them.

Similarly, in radio, the trick is to create word pictures that the natural sounds will enhance. "You don't need to say 'The early morning air was filled with the sound of cows' if you can actually hear the cows," explains Robert Smith. "You can say 'He reached into the fridge . . . ,' and if the next sound you hear is a can of beer being opened, you know what happened." As in television writing, when it comes to writing to sound, less is better.

And how do you match pictures and sounds to your words? A good rule of thumb is to use your strongest element for the beginning of your piece and the second-strongest to end your piece. Starting with the strongest sound or image gives you the best shot at attracting a viewer's attention. Of course, there are exceptions—there may be a picture that is not necessarily the second-best but which lends itself to being the closing, such as a sunset, someone leaving, or a beauty shot. If there's a logical closing shot or closing sound, then use it.

BROADCAST LEDES. Armed with an outline, we and most correspondents we know will try to write a piece from beginning to end, starting with the most important part: the lede. As in print, the point of the broadcast lede is to hook the listener, often with the most important or compelling point. "I don't personally believe in backing into a story. I think you need to grab them right at the top, especially in this day and age," says Lin Garlick of CBS Newspath. "The average news story is a minute thirty, so you can't mess around."

The typical broadcast lede is much shorter than the average print lede—just one sentence of ten to twenty words, usually—and it gets its power from working along with the video. Consider Elizabeth Palmer's lede on a story about the debut of the Airbus 380 superjet:

> No plane has ever been unveiled with more fanfare or dry ice.

The video showed blue clouds dancing around a large stage, masking the giant plane. Or take this lede by Steve Hartman of CBS News, one of the snappiest writers currently working in television. This story was about people growing pumpkins the size of automobiles:

> Call them "gourds gone wild."

These kinds of indirect ledes don't really give you the details, but they do pique your interest. After all, you can't tell the whole story in the lede. But if you make someone care about your story or at least start paying attention, you have done your job. "Make sure the lede has something in it that makes the story it introduces worth the viewer's time to watch it," advises James Ford. "The fact is that I can put together the best story imaginable, and it will mean very little if the viewer hears no reason in the lede (and, for that matter, the tease before the lede) to stick around and watch it." *Teases* are the little explanations that correspondents or anchors do to tell viewers what's coming up later in a program. They're like mini advertisements, aimed at keeping the viewer tuned in, and nearly every television news show has them and tries to make them enticing.

The broadcast lede, like the print lede, has to make the story seem exciting and revelant. "Recently I spoke with a writer about the importance of making sure the lede is addressed to you, the viewer," says Ford. "It doesn't necessarily have to use the word *you* (although that often helps), but it should be written with this question in mind: why should you care about the story the lede is leading into?" If they don't care, viewers may change the channel. So keep your lede concise, punchy, and powerful. Going back to our post office fire, here's how a good lede might look.

You might start with video of the damage with a lede directed directly to the viewer:

> (Postal workers carry out pile of dripping letters)
> If you're expecting something in the mail, you may be out of luck.

The lede explains what you see in the picture but doesn't repeat what you can see. It makes the story relevant to a local person by explaining that there will be a problem with mail delivery.

Or you can start with the pictures of the fire:

(Fire burns—smoke pours from post office)
Thousands of letters went up in smoke.

This, too, explains the picture without telling you what you can see. It aims at getting viewers wondering if their letters fed the flames and burned up, without using the word *you*. It's short and punchy.

If you watch any news broadcast, you'll see that almost every story starts with a punchy line. Sometimes you may see a lede of two sentences, both of which are short and snappy, like this lede from Russ Mitchell about the cost of running sports events:

Hoopla around Indiana high school basketball has been a tradition for generations. What's new is a growing sense of danger surrounding the games.

You probably wouldn't be able to write a two-sentence lede in a 1:30 story, but you can use ledes like this for longer stories. Sometimes you just can't make the impact you want in one line.

ANCHOR INTROS. And here's another difference from print: when you're writing that lede, be sure not to repeat what the anchor will say to lead into your story. Remember that there will almost always be an anchor who introduces your report, and you don't want your first sentence to step on the introduction, or vice versa. To do this, either write the introduction yourself, or just imagine what the anchor will say. "A good radio reporter always writes the host lede first," says Smith. "And you have to make it good enough so that a host will actually read it." Then don't repeat it—jump off from it. Continue the story from there. "My goal is always to try to begin in the middle of the story, the middle of the action," explains Smith. "If possible, I try to only say a few sentences before you hear something: a sound, a person talking, and exclamation. The pace on NPR can get slow sometimes, so I want to speed it up. The beginning should send the message, 'Something amazing is happening; let's go!'" When Beth is writing, especially for radio, she often writes the story from the beginning and then deletes the very first sentence or two, to make sure she gets right into the action and doesn't step on what the anchor will say.

FIVE FACTS. Once you're happy with the lede and have figured out the format, try to draft the body of the piece. In addition to the basic questions of journalism, the five Ws and an H, try to add other facts that give detail, background, and context. "I like to isolate the five really important facts I want to bring out," says Lin Garlick. "And then I want them put in order. So you start off with this, it grabs you, and then you segue to this, and then you segue to the next point, and segue to the next point." For a longer story, you might be able to make more than five points, but in the typical 1:30 long story, five points are about all you can fit in and explain.

Remember that in the last chapter, we talked about using your top five points in the top 10 percent of your print piece? Because a broadcast script is so much shorter than a newspaper or magazine piece, what would be the top 10 percent of a print piece is enough to fill a script. As we mentioned above, if you were to typeset the text for a two-minute-long television piece, it would fill just a few paragraphs.

Once you've identified the five points in your television or radio story, try to present them in a logical order, weaving the narration and the quotes together. The narration should make assertions that the quotes bear out. Try to write pieces of your story using what we'll call the *broadcast triad*—one or more sentences that make a statement, one sentence about that same idea that leads into a quote, and then the quotation itself. This should sound vaguely like the print triad we talked about in the last chapter, because they're both out to accomplish the same thing—assertion, proof, and attribution. You can repeat the broadcast triad as many times as necessary as you work through the ideas of your piece. Then add an ending and you've pretty much got your piece written. Increase the number and length of the quotes if you're doing a profile or a feature, and rely less on quotes if you're doing a complicated story that requires more explanation.

LINKING. The best television scripts, like the best radio scripts, skillfully interweave natural sound, narration, and sound bites into a smoothly flowing whole. Each sentence needs to be linked to the next, whether it's a sound bite or a piece of narration. Imagining ellipsis points between each phrase or sentence may help you achieve this effect. The easiest way to create links is to continue to refer to something that you just heard in a quote when you write the next line of narration, like in these examples:

Quote: "We've served tens of thousands of loyal customers, and it will be hard to tell them goodbye."

Narration: But goodbye it will be, when the Smith's Amusement Park closes for good tomorrow.

Quote: "I guess all good things must end someday, but I never thought they would tear down this amusement park."

Narration: But they will tear it down starting next week . . . to make room for a new shopping mall.

Or take this example from Mike's 2008 interview with Roger Clemens.

WALLACE: Were you to pass a lie detector test, would that help prove that you're telling the truth?
CLEMENS: Would it?
WALLACE: I don't know.
CLEMENS: I don't either.
NARRATION: And he doesn't know if he'll ever pitch again.

If you can't continue the idea of the quote, then use linking words to continue onward: words such as *but*, *and*, *still*, *meanwhile*, or *yet*. You can also link sound to words, like this:

Sound: (Park's theme song playing on loudspeaker at entrance)

Narration: That's the sound that's been greeting visitors to Smith's Amusement Park for more than seventy years.

You can also refer to the pictures to help things move along. In fact, you *should* refer to your pictures, especially when people might not know exactly what they're seeing. You can, for example, show a set of closed doors and say, "The school board is meeting behind these doors." That adds to the video rather than just explaining what viewers can already see. Referring to the pictures may also help your viewers follow along. "I'm a reporter on a morning news show, so we broadcast to people while they're getting dressed or grabbing breakfast or otherwise not looking at the screen," explains James Ford, "so I will frequently refer to my video in my script: 'This man, Joe Schmoe, police say caused the deadliest crash in Westchester County in seventy-five years. As you see from the burned-out wreckage . . . ,' as opposed to 'Police say Joe Schmoe caused the deadliest crash in Westchester County in seventy-five years.'" The difference made by referencing the pictures is subtle but is helpful to the viewer.

BEING CLEVER. Another big part of good broadcast writing is to use puns and plays on words that relate to the theme of the story. That helps make the story more interesting. In a story on church bell ringing, for example, Elizabeth Palmer explained that students had to go to school to "learn the ropes." Or take Beth's story on the World Toilet Organization (yes, it's real), which held its annual meeting in Moscow. "Toilets are a subject that may make people giggle, but it's heady stuff," she wrote. "The work of the WTO isn't likely to go to waste." These kinds of word plays shouldn't necessarily make you groan or even smile, but they should make the writing more lively. To do this, brainstorm about words that are somehow related to the subject of your story. Use a thesaurus to help you out if necessary, or a website where you can search for phrases using certain key words. You don't want to stretch too much to get those words in, but it makes the script stronger when you can fit in a few puns. But don't go too far and stretch it to something clichéd or inappropriate, such as something involving race, gender, or sexual orientation.

As in print, be a wordsmith. The beauty of your words still matters in broadcast writing. And just one word or phrase can make a huge difference in the way a piece feels. In particular, use verbs—strong verbs work best. You hear anchors say things like, "Men behaving badly in Colesville." That's not high-quality writing for broadcast journalism. A more grammatical way to say that would be, "Men are behaving badly in Colesville." Writing without verbs is bad. So is using clichés. In broadcasting it is very easy to be unoriginal or to whip out some overused phrase such as, "Only time will tell." Fight those impulses. Also, be sure not to put too much hype into your writing. Not every story has to be "exclusive." Not every crime has to be "horrific." Present the story without exaggeration and let your audience decide for themselves what they think. And as always, keep your personal feelings out of your writing. Watch out not only for obvious opinions but also for loaded words.

THE ENDING. A broadcast story doesn't just stop. It has to have an ending, or at least to come to rest at a logical place, which gives a conclusion and feeling of finality. "I think if you tell a story well enough, you don't have to manufacture an ending. There's a natural end point," explains Garlick. It may take some effort to get that goodbye correct. Ending on a quote is weak. It's better to end on a line of track, because the reporter should shape the last idea in a piece, which will remain in the audience's mind. "You want something that maybe makes you think of the larger picture, what the whole piece means," says NPR's Smith. "Often I'll try to dwell on a detail that seems symbolic, and just read it so it sounds conclusive."

Finding a good ending is often difficult. "I try to come up with a good line early in the process and save it for the end," Smith says. "On deadline, you are writing fast, and by the end there's nothing left to say but 'Only time will tell' or 'The draft environmental impact statement gets released in June.' These two forms make up probably half of the endings on NPR." And it's even harder to write an ending for television, where you need to match the ending text to an appropriate picture when you edit, so that the words and video will combine and give the desired impression. The point is to leave your audience with food for thought, but to do so without adding opinion.

FINISHING A SCRIPT. Once you have a first draft, read it aloud if you haven't already. Time it. Listen to the words as they come out. What looked good on paper but was hard to say? What sounds awkward? Can you condense? Even replacing two words with one is an improvement. Can you add alliteration, where several words begin with the same sound? That typical feature of broadcast writing makes things sound better as long as you don't overdo it. Can you be more clever? If you have time, try to incorporate additional thematic words and phrases into your script. Then pass your script on to your colleagues for a look. The people who have worked on the story with you make the best first readers. Then give the script to a superior for approval. A good editor who looks at things with fresh eyes can often make your script even better.

All television is educational television.
The question is: what is it teaching?

—NICHOLAS JOHNSON, former FCC commissioner

Assembling Your Report

Last comes the physical editing, or assembly, when you turn your script and pictures into a finished piece. The narration has to be recorded and then the whole report compiled. Editing in both radio and television is now done digitally, which makes the whole process simpler and faster than it was when tapes were involved. It used to be that pictures and sound were copied during the editing process from one tape to another in a linear fashion. If you wanted to add something to the middle, you had to rerecord part of what you had already done, which was annoying and time-consuming. Nonlinear editing has made life much easier—now it just takes a few clicks of a mouse to put down the pictures or move them around.

Because of digital editing, reporters are increasingly expected to be able to edit their pieces themselves. Old-fashioned physical editing required specialists, but nonlinear editing is not that difficult to learn, and the necessary software can be loaded onto almost any laptop computer. Computer-based editing is a fantastic skill to learn if you're serious about becoming a journalist.

No matter which system you use to edit, there are some basic rules to follow:

The pictures and the words must match in television, and the sound and words must match in radio. If you're talking about one thing but showing or hearing another, your viewers are almost certain to become confused. In television, if you say it, show it. The pictures are stronger than the words. If the words say one thing but the pictures say another, then the pictures will win. And that makes for bad television. For example, if you say that the president's popularity ratings are dropping, but show a campaign rally where people are going crazy for him, your words will be overwhelmed by the pictures.

You need a certain amount of pictures to do a good story. You must have enough video to cover what you are writing. Trying to edit a piece when you lack enough material is a recipe for mediocrity. If you're short on picture, then try to shoot, buy, or borrow more material.

Your timing matters. Your narration has to work along with the pictures and sound, and often has to be timed to the images and sounds in your report to work. It can be hard to synchronize your words and the pictures, but when they work together they allow for people to hear and see together. Consider this line of track: "After a gastric bypass, Lucy Smith went from this . . . to this." If the pictures of her before and after don't appear at the right moments, the meaning will be lost.

Sometimes it's best to let the pictures and sound speak for themselves. It's tempting to talk and talk, but sometimes viewers just want to watch or listen to what's happening. Reports can benefit from just letting the pictures and sound run.

Natural sound is important in television, too. The tendency in television is to focus on images, but TV works best when the natural sound works along with the pictures and narration. If you really pay attention when you watch television, you'll notice there are frequent breaks in the narration for natural sound. These are called *natural sound breaks*. As we have said, sound is not just for radio.

Don't forget that what you are ultimately doing is telling a story. When you're done with your edit, look at it and ask yourself if you have covered the who, what, where, when, why, how, so what, and what's next. Ask if the typical person will understand your story. Don't be afraid to revise or edit to make your report better, especially if you notice a problem in the finished piece that you didn't anticipate.

Double-check that you got your best material into the edited story. Journalists sometimes get so focused on the words that they forget to make sure their best pictures and sound get into a piece. Don't let that happen to you. Create a system for yourself to make sure the best material doesn't end up on a shelf instead of in your report.

Value the opinion of your colleagues. Broadcasting is a collaborative art. Make sure you seek out and incorporate the opinions of your teammates.

A fine quotation is a diamond in the hand of a man of wit and a pebble in the hand of a fool.

—JOSEPH ROUX, French artist

Lead-ins and Attribution in Broadcasting

In radio, you must be particularly careful in the way you write into quotes: if you don't introduce the speaker before each quote, there's no way for your listeners to know who is speaking. Even if there's only one other person besides the reporter speaking in the piece, listeners may not be paying close attention or may be just tuning in, so you have to remind them who is talking each time you use a sound bite. The first time, introduce the speaker with a full name and title, as in "Colesville mayor John Smith says taxes are already too high." But on subsequent mentions, your attribution can be as simple as saying "Mayor Smith" before his sound bite, with the intonation indicating that it's his quotation.

Professional radio reporters do sometimes put in a short sound bite without introducing the speaker first. That's a stylistic choice that can also get the listener's attention. You hear a quote and think, "Well, who said that?" Then the narration has to tell you who you just heard. This technique of delaying the identification of the speaker usually works only if there will be a second, longer sound bite that follows the first, teasing sound bite.

And here's another special requirement for radio: give the source of your information early on in each sentence where you need attribution. "Police say Joe Shmoe extorted one million dollars from his next-door neighbor," not "Joe Shmoe extorted one million dollars from his next door neighbor, police say." You want viewers to know up front where your information is coming from. Don't make them wait for it.

SUPERS. In television, attribution is slightly different because you have more tools at your disposal—like a *super* (also called a *chyron*, pronounced "KAI-ron"), which can put someone's name and title on the screen. That means you do not necessarily have to mention someone's name or title in the lead-in to a sound bite the way you have to in radio. But if there's going to be a super on-screen, then make an accommodation for one when filming. You lose about the bottom 20 percent of the frame to the super. So when you shoot an interview, frame your interviewee to account for the super (and also for the crawl—those words scrolling across the bottom of the screen—if your station has one). Leave extra space at the interview subject's chest level, so the super won't block his or her face. You also need to consider the length of your quotation before deciding whether to use a super. You usually need at least a four-second-long sound bite to put someone's name and title on-screen, because viewers need time to read. You should also know in advance whether your show uses supers—some, such as *CBS News Sunday Morning*, don't allow them.

I would listen to how they told the story,
to what elements they used, to how it sounded,
and that's who I patterned myself after,
the people who were on CBS News.

—ED BRADLEY, journalist

Reading for Broadcast

In our converged media environment, every journalist should be able to read a radio report or podcast. The same is true of television, although you need a whole other set of skills if you are going to appear on camera, such as the ability to speak without moving your head and hands too much. (Try it. It may be harder than you think!) Some people are blessed with wonderful voices, and that certainly makes it easier to read a television or radio report. But some people with average voices have made it in the industry because they have learned to use their talents to the maximum. Here are a few tips for reading for broadcast:

Don't rush. Don't be tempted to read quickly to get more information across. If you sound rushed, it hampers your listeners' ability to absorb information. Read slowly. Cut out material if you can't make it in time.

Sound conversational. Forget about that fake-sounding, smarmy broadcasting voice you might know from the movies. Professional broadcasters try to sound serious but not over the top. Remember, you broadcast to just one person at a time.

Don't read in a monotone. Whenever you read for broadcast, give some words additional emphasis. This is called *punching* your script. Punch the most important words in your script to help them stand out. Reporters often underline the words they want to punch, or type them in all capital letters. That keeps your voice from staying too level and sounding boring. "When we read on the air, we're trying to change the sounds of our voices—sometimes questioning, sometimes authoritative, sometimes amused or sad," says Robert Smith. That makes listening more enjoyable.

Pauses are your friend. Use them for emphasis—more so on public radio, less so on commercial radio or TV. Good broadcast reporters use a lot of dashes or ellipsis points when writing their scripts so that they'll know where to pause and how to read the phrases properly. Use punctuation to help you read, like this: "Barbara Walters . . . one of journalism's most famous interviewers . . . has just released her autobiography."

Cadence is important, too. Think of your script as a musical score and your voice as an instrument. For example, you can read high in your register, in the middle of it, or low in your register. In general, women should read low in their register and men high in their register to sound authoritative.

Think about when you want to breathe—either at the end of a sentence or at the end of a phrase. Some reporters actually write where to breathe right on their scripts. You never want to sound breathless. If you're gasping for air, it may be a sign that your sentences are too long.

Write the way you need to read. Make sure you spell out abbreviations the way they are pronounced, like Y-M-C-A (letters spoken individual) or NATO (spoken as a word). Write out difficult words or names phonetically, such as "Illinois governor Rod Blagojevich (bla-GOY-a-vich)." Write numbers and figures the way you will read them, like "750 billion dollars," not "$750 billion."

Television saved the movies. The Internet is going to save the news business.

—MATT DRUDGE, journalist and author

How News Works on the Internet

Although there are some good reporting sites that exist only on the Internet, including Slate, Talking Points Memo, and Daily Kos, a lot of the best journalism on the Net is still coming from the mainstream media, at least right now. But Internet-only news sites will continue to gain audience—and to be truly useful, they'll have to adhere to the same standards for integrity as old media. It's critical for users to know that what they're reading online is true and has been verified. "Our priorities are accuracy, speed, and finding stories or angles on stories that other news outlets are missing," says Joshua Micah Marshall, the founder, editor, and publisher of the Talking Points Memo (TPM) websites. "Accuracy, being fundamentally honest with readers, proper sourcing all remain the same" as with traditional media, he says.

Despite these similarities, Marshall says that Internet news sites such as his try to do some things a little bit differently than traditional media to take advantage of the strengths of the medium. "What we've tried to do is develop a style of reporting that is native to the Web and to the greatest degree we can exploit its advantages and mitigate its shortcomings," he says. "Most of that is what we call an 'iterative' style of reporting, in which we cover a story not in a self-contained set piece but as a stream of posts, going on for hours, days, weeks, which covers a story in its totality over time." That reporting style has brought the site attention and accolades. Talking Points Memo started out in late 2000 as a site about the Florida presidential vote recount (when it wasn't clear who had won Florida, George W. Bush or Al Gore). But it soon expanded into politics in general, and has done some great reporting. Marshall was honored with one of journalism's top honors, a 2007 George Polk Award, for an investigation into the Bush administration's politically motivated firing of eight U.S. attorneys. "Marshall's tenacious investigative reporting sparked interest by the traditional news media and led to the resignation of Attorney General Alberto Gonzales," said the award citation. The Polk is proof that Internet journalism can be first-rate and serve the very highest calling.

The most important difference between Internet reporting and reporting in other media is that Internet journalism is *immediate*. You can post something to a website very quickly, as opposed to having to wait for a paper to be printed or a news broadcast to come on the air. That's often good if you're a news consumer, but it can be bad if you're a news producer. The Internet has turned almost all reporters into something akin to wire service reporters by demanding constant updates of the news. "In the last couple years the trend has been more mainstream news organizations moving toward the mode of iterative reporting I described above," Marshall says. Even though a newspaper still prints only once a day, readers now expect the paper's website to be updated round the clock with the latest news.

It used to be that reporters for major newspapers had to write a story only once a day. They'd work all day and sometimes into the night, submit a story for deadline, and then do it all again the next day. That model is all but gone. Reporters for newspapers now have to file stories whenever breaking news happens. "Instead of spending all day running around town reporting stories, making phone calls, and doing research, on a breaking news story I now may have to produce two or more Web versions of the story throughout the day," explains Kim Murphy of the *Los Angeles Times*. "Then, at the end of the day, the paper expects something different, a second-day approach or analysis that goes beyond just the facts on the Web, for the print edition. This doubles your workload and leaves you far less time for collecting the details and nuances that go into the well-crafted story you would have done in the old days." This is a change that doesn't make everyone very happy. "The advent of the Web should have brought *more* staff to do both jobs," says Murphy. "Instead, we are doing twice the work with half the people."

Reporter Anthony Ramirez notes that because of the pace demanded by the Internet, there's no longer time to check out the press releases and other information that is passed along to the paper. "Typically, whether metro or financial, some story will begin with a handout, usually written in gobbledygook," he says. "Before the Internet, I'd call up somebody knowledgeable and ask what the handout means, maybe read it to him, get a quick assessment, then start interviewing in earnest," he explains. That sort of reporting would take only about an hour, but Ramirez says that became too long to wait in the Internet era. "Now I'm supposed to throw the gobbledygook on the Web instantly, with no assessment. That's not what the *New York Times* used to do, but it's what it does now because that's what drives traffic for the website," he says.

The Internet has also changed how broadcast channels work. Reporters at broadcast channels such as ABC, NBC, and CBS used to be able to wait for hours before producing a report if they didn't have a show going on soon. Say something happened at noon but the network didn't have a news show until 6:30 p.m. That gave the journalists time to think, report, and craft a piece. But now networks have to create video reports for their websites whenever big news breaks, even if it's hours before the network's next news broadcast goes on the air. That gives consumers the news faster, but means the report may not be very good.

"What I often say is that I'm delighted that I'm not there today, because I'm not sure that I could do it," confesses Marvin Kalb, the former CBS and NBC News correspondent. "If I didn't feel comfortable, fully comfortable, with a fact, I'm not sure that I ever would've gone on the air with it." Just as the Internet is transforming newspapers into wire services, it's transforming regular broadcast news operations into 24/7 cable-style news channels, delivering news round the clock on the Internet. Quality and fact checking inevitably suffer.

We also wonder whether the process of reading online makes it more difficult for people to keep their attention on longer texts such as books. Some people are now used to absorbing only a few screenfuls of information at a time, and start to zone out if they have to read too much of one thing. That makes it more important than ever to hook readers at the start of a story.

But there are real advantages to the Internet as well. "The level of research you can do on anything is just so deep," says Jill Abramson, managing editor of the *New York Times*. "Just the *Times* site alone—if you get going on our Topics pages, you can be reading forever, and learning the total background of any subject."

The Internet also creates a wonderful way to present more journalism online than could ever fit in a paper, magazine, or broadcast. Take the PBS documentary about Iraq entitled *Bush's War*, which aired as part of the series *Frontline* in 2008. The producers not only posted the whole two-part documentary online but also provided links to more than four hundred full interviews with government officials, experts, and other people interviewed by *Frontline* on subjects relating to Iraq. Those interviews would take days and days to view, but by posting them online instead of keeping them in the PBS archives, those interviews become accessible to everyone. And that's wonderful. Mike's early interviews from ABC from 1957 and 1958 are available on the Web instead of sitting in some vault somewhere. The other thing the Net does very well is to give access to original documents that might be time-consuming or difficult to access otherwise.

We also like the idea of what's called open-source reporting—which is when you appeal to your audience for story ideas and help with ongoing stories. This is obviously a great way to bring in new information from the people who are most affected by news. Equally revolutionary is the way eyewitnesses to news events now have easy ways to share their photos and videos with journalists. But (as in any other medium) it makes both of us uncomfortable if people who help are paid for their information, because it may create incentives for people to lie. That's the kind of ethical issue we will address in more detail in the next chapter.

And we like that the Internet creates an easy way for people to comment on stories and to communicate with reporters. Sometimes people just rant and rave, but other times they add interesting personal observations or professional opinion. And it's useful for reporters to be able to gauge what people think of their reports. "I'm lucky that most *New York Times* readers are fairly literate and temperate, with the exception of anything involving Israel," says Ramirez about receiving feedback. One CBS News correspondent we know recently sent out an e-mail to the entire staff pointing out that one of his blog entries about health care had garnered hundreds of very interesting comments. If one of those comments then spurs more reporting, even better.

What does all this mean for journalists starting out today? Young journalists need to be thinking creatively about how to maximize the Web's benefits. Consider how you can use the Internet to add value to the reporting that is already available. Can you put your full interviews on the Web? Might you create a timeline? What about a quiz? In this age of short attention spans, you also need to think about how to use different kinds of graphics to portray and simplify complex information. If you're not strong in this suit, check out the works of Edward Tufte, a retired Yale professor who has written several brilliant books about displaying information graphically and who's been called one of the most influential graphic designers of our times.

Clearly, all journalists must know how to use the Internet as a basic tool for reporting. But the more creative you can be in conceiving ways in which the Internet can add new layers of value to your reporting, the more likely you are to prove yourself useful in the converged world.

6

THE SOUL OF JOURNALISM: LAW AND ETHICS

Ethics is knowing the difference between what you have a right to do and what is right to do.

—POTTER STEWART, U.S. Supreme Court justice

If you've followed the news in the past few years, you've likely read coverage of some mind-boggling ethical lapses by reporters. The people in this rogues' gallery have shaken the very foundation of journalism. There was Jayson Blair, a young reporter for the *New York Times*, who fabricated at least three dozen stories. He lied about taking reporting trips—staying in New York when he said he was elsewhere covering stories—made up material, and plagiarized for months before being caught. Then there was Jack Kelley of *USA Today*, who not only made up parts of his stories for more than a decade but even asked his friends to pose as sources for editors who were calling to fact-check, so he wouldn't get caught breaking the rules. And at CBS News, a scandal over memos purporting to show that George W. Bush received preferential treatment as a young airman during the Vietnam War nearly ended the careers of the network's main anchor, Dan Rather, and four of his colleagues. The memos about Bush were never ascertained to be real, and the whole CBS News system for maintaining accuracy seemed to malfunction. These are very extreme cases, of course, but their existence demonstrates the importance of having a firm grounding in ethics and the law. To succeed, reporters need to be governed by what is moral as well as what is legal.

The Essentials of Ethics

News organizations take ethics very seriously. Most mainstream organizations have lengthy written standards that set the tone for journalists' behavior, and they need them, because virtually all journalists we know have faced ethical issues in their work. We certainly have. "I remember covering the opening of a mobile phone store in Moscow, and they were handing out expensive phones to all the journalists," remembers Beth. "My crew and I were the only ones who didn't take them, much to the surprise of the store's PR rep, but I explained that CBS News has rules against taking gifts. I probably would have gotten away with it, but it just wasn't worth jeopardizing my career for a $500 phone." Websites may not have written rules of conduct, but most traditional media do, and not just for show. "We try to apply a set of standards," explains the top editor at the *New York Times*, Bill Keller. "Newspapers are put out by human beings, so we don't do any of this perfectly, but we attempt to present it [the news] in as fair and accurate a way as we can."

Journalists are supposed to adhere to ethical rules not only to safeguard their own careers but also to protect the reputation and livelihood of their organizations. News media aren't usually put out of business by ethical or legal gaffes, but such problems can erode the audience's trust, which in turn can lead to losses in audience, advertising, and the ability of the news outlet to get other people to agree to interviews. Many people already believe that the media are biased and unfair, and each time an ethical lapse happens, they can point their finger and say, "See? I told you so!" So ethics and law form the framework under which journalism becomes credible.

It's difficult to categorize the kinds of ethical dilemmas journalists tend to face, because they often cross several areas. But here's an overview of the issues journalists meet most frequently. (Yes, many of these will sound obvious, but people still get in trouble for crossing these lines every day. They're worth emphasizing.)

PLAGIARISM. Journalists sometimes quote one another, or reuse quotes that other journalists have gathered. As long as the source of the material is included, that's not plagiarism. Very rarely, reporters simply take someone else's material and try to pass it off as their own. That *is* plagiarism. One of the last things Jayson Blair did before being fired from the *New York Times* was to plagiarize an article from a Texas newspaper about a family whose soldier son was missing in Iraq. The original story said this about the mother in the family: "She points to the pinstriped couches, the tennis bracelet still in its red velvet case and the Martha Stewart patio furniture." Blair's piece, which ran eight days later, read: "Juanita Angiano points proudly to the pinstriped couches, the tennis bracelet in its red case and the Martha Stewart furniture out on the patio." When the author of the first story saw Blair's version, she alerted her editor, who called the *Times*. A team of *Times* reporters investigated and found not only that Blair had never interviewed this woman but that he had lied habitually. He was fired and discredited, ending his career in journalism. Blair later said in an autobiography that his deceptions were inspired by a desperate desire to get his articles into the newspaper, as well as such personal problems as cocaine use, alcohol abuse, and manic-depression.

The Internet has made plagiarism a lot easier—a few strokes are all you need to copy and paste. But the Net has also made it much easier to catch this kind of behavior. In the pre-Net days, to look for pilfered content you would have to get a hard copy of a newspaper either at the library or at a special newsstand that carried out-of-town papers. Now you can do so easily online. And there are also several good software programs that check for plagiarism.

FABRICATION. Let's say you're getting reactions from people outside your office building to a news event—a form of newsgathering that journalists call *vox pop* or *MOS* (man on the street). If you make something up, you may think that no one will ever know. But you'd be surprised how quickly a seasoned editor can pick out a fabricated quote. And what if your editor asks to hear your tape of the man-on-the-street interviews? Not having one may raise even more suspicion. Or what if you interview a real person but make up something he or she said? That may even be worse ethically, because the source now has to take responsibility for something he or she did not actually say. That's a major ethical violation.

The most famous journalistic fabrication of recent years involved Janet Cooke, a reporter for the *Washington Post*. Her 1980 story "Jimmy's World," about an eight-year-old heroin addict in Washington, D.C., won a Pulitzer Prize. But it so hurt the image of the District of Columbia that its mayor, Marion Barry, had officials scour the city, looking for child drug addicts. After none was found, Cooke admitted that "Jimmy" was a fabrication. She resigned from the paper and returned the Pulitzer. Cooke's career was ruined, and the *Post*'s reputation took a beating.

MANIPULATION. There have been several famous ethics cases where a journalistic organization secretly manipulated something to get a certain result. The most famous case of this sort happened in 1992, when the newsmagazine *Dateline NBC* investigated the safety of the fuel tanks on some General Motors trucks in a segment entitled "Waiting to Explode." The program showed a frightening video in which the fuel tank on a GM pickup exploded after a side collision with another car at low speed. Only it turned out that the crash testers NBC News used had rigged the explosion with small incendiary devices, because they couldn't get it to happen any other way. General Motors sued NBC News, and the two eventually settled out of court. Despite the settlement, the incident formed a dark blotch on the network's reputation. Not only did NBC News apologize on air, but its president resigned as a result.

You also can't manipulate people so that they say exactly what you want them to say. "You can't put words in peoples' mouth," says Linda Mason, the ethics guru for CBS News. "Sometimes you have done a lot of preparation and you have talked to your interviewees and they say great things on the phone, and you get to the interview and they don't say anything. You can't say, 'Well, last night when we talked, you said this and this and this. Can you say this again?'" That's the journalistic equivalent of leading a witness during a trial, and really not allowed. An interview subject may object to a leading question and say, "Hey, don't put words in my mouth, please," but usually it's up to journalists to self-police for that kind of behavior.

A trickier area of manipulation lies in slanting a story to produce a particular editorial result. Editors often have specific ideas about the kinds of stories they want, and sometimes those ideas can clash with what a reporter's actually found. "*Fortune* magazine wanted me to remove all references to racism in a cover story about Asian American business executives because they wanted a 'success' story and only a success story," remembers Anthony Ramirez, who worked at the magazine from 1985 to 1989. "The editors also wanted a small sidebar speculating that Asians may be genetically superior," which was something Ramirez did not feel comfortable writing. He did it, but he was so angry that he started looking for another job the following week and soon left the magazine.

PRIVACY. Should the victim of a crime be named publicly? What about someone underage who commits a crime? Should someone's sexual preference be made public? What about other personal information? Many news organizations have guidelines for dealing with privacy issues, such as whether to use the name of a victim of sexual assault or a juvenile offender. But the guidelines may not address all real-life situations. Consider the 2009 documentary film *Outrage*, which investigated members of Congress who oppose gay rights and claimed that many were secretly homosexual themselves. The film caused an ethical issue for film reviewers, who had to weigh whether to mention the names of the members of Congress featured in the film. Some reviews did, while others did not.

Or consider the Chicago Cubs fan Steve Bartman, who interfered with a foul ball during the 2003 National League Championship Series. He cost the Cubs an out, and they then lost that game, and eventually the series. Chicago newspapers were faced with a dilemma: print the fan's name and hometown, knowing he might be harmed, or not? Most of them did, no doubt aided by the fact that Bartman's name was out on the Internet in minutes.

Also, journalists sometimes get hold of newsworthy information that is essentially private, such as e-mail correspondence, telephone conversations, or voice mail, and have to decide whether to use it or not. Such was the case in June 2009 after reporters discovered that the governor of South Carolina, Mark Sanford, had a mistress in Argentina. After the affair became public, the *State*, a newspaper in Columbia, South Carolina, printed a few of the e-mails between the governor and his lover—e-mails it had obtained the previous year but had not published, because editors couldn't confirm that they were real.

But beware, because journalists have been punished for using material obtained illegally. Michael Gallagher, a reporter for the *Cincinnati Enquirer*, wrote twenty-two stories alleging wrongdoing by the Cincinnati-based fruit company Chiquita Brands International, all published on one day in 1998. The stories accused the company of unethical behavior in Latin America, including ignoring local laws, bribing officials, and using pesticides on its workers. The articles were based on thousands of company voice mails that Gallagher initially said had been leaked to him by a source inside the company but which he actually obtained by accessing the voice mail system himself, apparently with the help of someone from Chiquita. The paper retracted the stories and paid millions of dollars in damages to Chiquita. Gallagher not only was fired but later was charged with two felonies.

People who think their privacy has been invaded can sue, and the courts have generally upheld the right to privacy. The courts have defined four different types of invasion of privacy: intrusion into one's home or property, the public disclosure of private facts, publishing private information that paints someone in a false light (this is a bit different from libel or slander, which we will discuss more in a moment), and the appropriation of someone's image without his or her permission.

So when deciding how to treat issues that deal with privacy, journalists need to consider both legal issues and professional ethics. And ethical standards vary somewhat among news outlets. For instance, the entire industry of celebrity news thrives on getting the kind of inside information that may violate, or come close to violating, someone's privacy. Some other publications have made it a particular point to "out" gay politicians and celebrities.

News organizations differ so much in their aims, and real-life situations vary so much, that it makes it difficult to come up with rules for deciding whether to report something that might violate someone's privacy. The only rule is that decisions involving privacy have to be made by the reporters and editors at each news organization, along with their attorneys, with full consideration given to ethical concerns and possible legal consequences.

INVOLVEMENT WITH SOURCES. We've already written about how journalists benefit from building relationships with their sources, and how sources can benefit from their relations with journalists. Sometimes relationships between reporters and the people they interview grow from professional associations into friendship or even love. That can make things complicated. Although journalists try to maintain objectivity, they can sometimes be affected by the relations they have with people involved in their stories. When there is a direct conflict, most journalists will remove themselves from a story. It's easy to see that you should not report about a town if, say, your husband becomes the mayor. But usually things are trickier than that. The catch-22 is that if you don't get close to your sources, you may not be getting much out of them—but if you get *too* close, it becomes difficult to cover a story objectively. That line between professional and personal can get awfully hard to see sometimes.

This is an issue Mike knows well, as he had close relations with President Richard Nixon. Mike covered Nixon during his runs for the White House in 1960 and 1968, and respected Nixon's intelligence and command of facts. "I remember one long conversation that we had, he and I, on an airplane going from Oregon to New York, in which we just sat side by side on the plane and shot the breeze," Mike remembers. "He was good in so many ways. He was so smart, so thoughtful, married to a wonderful woman, good kids, and I just simply found myself liking him." After Nixon won in 1968, he asked Mike to serve as his press secretary. Mike thought about the offer but declined, because he had recently started working for the new show *60 Minutes* and wanted to see where it would go.

Mike dealt with potential conflicts of interest by limiting the number of interviews he did with those he knew well, and by asking the same tough questions of his friends as he did of his enemies. Mike didn't cover Nixon's day-to-day activities after declining to work for him, but as Watergate unfolded, no one asked tougher questions of Nixon's key advisors than Mike did. In this case, professionalism meant putting aside any personal feeling about President Nixon and reporting the story, no matter where the facts took him.

Mike's relationship with Nixon was one of intellectual attraction. But what happens when there's a physical attraction?

That's what Kim Murphy says happened to her when she was covering the courts in Los Angeles and found herself drawn to one of the main lawyers whose cases she covered. "He had been a frequent source of news stories for me, and in an attempt to cultivate him as a source, I had frequently had dinner with him, when we invariably spent the evening talking about court cases and fascinating tidbits he knew about the federal judges and their various legal and personal histories. During the course of this 'source cultivation,' a mutual attraction developed," she recalls. "This was never even mentioned, until one time he had me stop by his apartment on my way back to my car after dinner and he hugged me as I was leaving. I realized it had somehow crossed an improper line. I told him so. He said he couldn't see how we were doing anything wrong. After that, the dinners stopped and I started covering his cases far less frequently, if indeed at all. It was a shame. My work was diminished because I was not getting the information from him I used to. I felt badly that it wouldn't have happened to a male reporter, who would have been able to continue to see the guy with impunity."

Some journalists in that same kind of position have lost their jobs for crossing the line with their sources, or been reassigned. For example, Suzy Wetlaufer was the editor of the *Harvard Business Review* in 2001 when she interviewed the chairman of General Electric, Jack Welch, for a profile. It didn't take long for the relationship to turn romantic, even though Welch was married. When it did, Wetlaufer informed her boss and asked that her article not be published. It wasn't—and she was fired. It all turned out okay for her in the end, perhaps because she did the ethical thing and disclosed the relationship before publication. Jack and Suzy Welch—they're married now—have written several best-selling books and write a weekly syndicated column. But there's a lesson there: if a relationship with a source does turn romantic, the best thing to do is to disclose it right away and ask for a reassignment.

The relations between sources and journalists are perhaps most highly charged when it comes to business, when millions may be lost or gained based on information being reported. Business journalists in particular are often sought out by the rich and powerful, and so reporters who cover business have to be extra careful to steer clear of personal relationships that might be inappropriate. They also have to be careful of people trying to make money by exploiting their connections by either placing or gathering some kind of commercial information. Most news organizations have strict rules against using any kind of inside information for material gain. Yet there can be a thin line between what's allowed and what's not. In 2007, Maria Bartiromo, a star reporter for the financial network CNBC, was accused of being too close to Citigroup in general, and to one Citigroup executive in particular. Bartiromo was criticized in the press, but CNBC stood behind her, perhaps because her role as the "Money Honey"—a nickname that was trademarked, by the way—made her too popular with viewers to lose. Interestingly enough, her career has continued to flourish, but the executive in question at Citigroup was fired and is now working somewhere else.

COMMERCIAL CONCERNS. Many news outlets are now owned either by large media companies or by conglomerates, and this creates conflicts of interest that can affect reporting. For example, Comcast owns a majority stake in NBC Universal. So how is NBC News to do an investigative piece about something that goes wrong at Comcast? That is a direct conflict of interest.

Of course, networks do report about the companies that own them—it's hard for a news organization to ignore a major news story that involves its parent. But the fact is, a newspaper or station is likely not going to investigate the company that owns it. It gets even more complicated when a media company controls many media outlets, such as Rupert Murdoch's News Corporation, which owns newspapers, magazines, television stations, cable networks, film studios, and a book publisher. Each part of a media empire such as Murdoch's is likely to give positive coverage to its sister companies. You can call that corporate synergy . . . or a recipe for flawed coverage.

There can also be conflicts in the relations between news organizations and their advertisers. Advertisers have been known to pull their ads when the publication or channel gives them less than glowing coverage. General Motors, for example, pulled its ads from the *Los Angeles Times* for about four months in 2005 to make clear its displeasure with some of the paper's editorial comments about GM vehicles. News companies can also be faced with a problem when one of their main advertisers is involved in bad news. Coverage of the problem may cause the advertiser to pull its ads, costing the news company thousands or even millions of dollars. Journalists may also be slow to do investigative stories about a major advertiser. And companies probably will not want to advertise on a channel or in a publication that has done an investigation of its business practices.

Another kind of dilemma occurs when a news organization is worried that an important, journalistically worthy story could get it into expensive legal trouble. A perfect example is the story Mike did about the tobacco industry, which became the basis for the film *The Insider*. Former tobacco executive Jeffrey Wigand gave Mike an exclusive interview in 1995 saying that his company, cigarette maker Brown & Williamson, knew that the nicotine in its cigarettes got smokers hooked, despite statements to the contrary, and knew that the chemicals contained in the cigarettes were harmful. It was the first time someone from inside the tobacco industry had spoken out about the deadly secrets of the trade. Mike had an amazing exposé, but CBS News executives almost killed the story over financial worries. By talking to *60 Minutes*, Wigand was violating the terms of his confidentiality agreement with Brown & Williamson, opening up CBS News to a potential lawsuit for millions or perhaps even billions of dollars.

Mike fought to show the interview despite the possible legal costs but was essentially overruled by his superiors. Instead, he ultimately did a watered-down report about cigarettes for *60 Minutes*, which closed with Mike stating on camera that CBS News was not allowing the whole story to be aired. It was only after the *Wall Street Journal* essentially assumed the risk of a lawsuit by publishing a story about Wigand, citing much the same information that he had told Mike first, that Mike's bosses relented and finally aired Mike's whole interview with the whistle-blower.

Mike is not proud of the incident, nor is he happy about how it was portrayed in *The Insider*. "The people who saw *The Insider* believed that our team had lost our moral compass," Mike says. "It wasn't true." (See Mike's earlier book *Between You and Me* for a fuller discussion of the fallout of the Wigand interview.)

COMPETITION-RELATED DILEMMAS. Sometimes journalists are put into a tough spot because they want to stay competitive. That means they may rush a story into print or onto the air when it's really not ready because they hear through the grapevine that a competitor has the story. (Even though news organizations try to keep their actions secret, a lot of gossiping across companies still goes on.) And running any story that hasn't been thoroughly checked for accuracy is a recipe for trouble. That's what happened to CBS News in 2004 when it ran the story dubbed "Memogate" on *60 Minutes II*. The story alleged that George W. Bush had received preferential treatment when serving in the Texas Air National Guard (TexANG) in 1972 and 1973. The proof of the allegations was six photocopied documents purporting to show that his superiors were pressured to improve Bush's record and exempt him from requirements of the job, such as a physical exam. The producer of the piece, Mary Mapes, not only procured the documents but was in charge of getting them authenticated.

A report issued months later by an independent review panel established by CBS News determined that Mapes and the correspondent, Dan Rather, had rushed the piece onto the air without ascertaining that the documents were real. In fact, the report had aired just six days after Mapes received the documents in question. She knew that other organizations were working on the same story and thought one of them was about to break it. She wanted CBS News to be first. "These problems were caused primarily by a myopic zeal to be the first news organization to broadcast what was believed to be a new story about President Bush's TexANG service, and the rigid and blind defense of the Segment after it aired despite numerous indications of its shortcomings," stated the report.

As we mentioned earlier, almost everyone involved in vetting the report was either fired or, like Rather, induced to leave CBS News. The scandal damaged CBS News' reputation. "Our checks and balances did not work. And since then we have revised our whole system," explains Linda Mason, who as senior vice president is in charge of ethics and standards at CBS News.

SECURITY CONCERNS. Journalists occasionally have to deal with a dilemma about publishing or broadcasting something that might endanger national security. This happens fairly rarely, but it does happen. And since the attacks of September 11, 2001, reporters have probably become a bit more attuned to national security concerns. In this type of dilemma, reporters have to weigh getting a big story against possible harm to the nation's defense interests.

The most famous story of this kind was the so-called Pentagon Papers case. The Pentagon Papers were a 7,000-plus-page history of the Vietnam War put together by the Defense Department in 1967–68. They were supposed to be classified, but a defense analyst got hold of them and leaked them to the *New York Times*. The newspaper started to publish them in 1971, but the government ordered the paper to stop, arguing that publication would damage national security. The case went all the way to the Supreme Court, and did so in record time. Ultimately, the justices ruled that the Pentagon Papers were not a threat to national security and could be published—but they also noted that the government could in principle keep the media from reporting something that would directly damage national security.

There are also special national security concerns during times of war. Journalists have accompanied troops into battle for as long as there have been journalists, but there have been more restrictions put upon journalists in recent years, as technology has changed. Many American journalists were embedded with the U.S. military during the Iraq invasion in 2003, and many more have been embedded with troops in both Iraq and Afghanistan since then. During an embed, reporters are usually not allowed by the U.S. military to report certain things that might create danger for the troops, such as their exact locations. Reporters agree to some degree of censorship in order to travel with U.S. forces. We think that the decision to embed leads to generally positive press coverage for the war effort from the embedded journalists, because the stationing of reporters with the troops subtly undermines the reporters' sense of objectivity. They eat, live, and travel with the troops—and depend on the soldiers for their personal safety—and that erodes some journalists' objective distance. We've heard more than one journalist use the word *we* when referring to the troops.

Another concern is journalists' safety. Journalists sometimes travel to dangerous places, and they can be kidnapped, injured, or even killed. That can also create an ethical dilemma. Take the case of *New York Times* reporter David Rohde, who was kidnapped with two Afghan colleagues in Afghanistan in 2008. Rohde was held for seven months, until he and his Afghan assistant were able to escape. Not only did the *Times* decide against reporting about Rohde's capture, but its editors convinced other news organizations to suppress the story until he got away. "It wasn't that difficult to keep it secret, because most other news organizations understood the arguments. Some of them had been through similar situations, and they understood the argument that going public with this could greatly increase the danger," explains *Times* editor Bill Keller. "The difficulty was kind of convincing ourselves that that was the right strategy, because we're a news organization. We don't like to sit on a story." Keller says that when Rohde was released, the reporter told him that maintaining secrecy about the story undoubtedly had helped keep them alive.

GIFTS. Many news organizations have strict rules against the practice of giving money or gifts to potential interview subjects, a practice known as *checkbook journalism*. The purpose of this is to ensure that sources have no financial incentive to lie or fabricate something.

Yet sometimes news organizations, particularly television stations, spar over guests—and so the guest can make certain financial requests. "There's an incredible amount of competition, especially in morning TV," says Russ Mitchell, the CBS News anchor. "It's pretty cutthroat. I've been places on breaking news stories where the competition has sent flowers to the person they want to interview, they've sent personal notes from the anchor who wants to interview them, who has promised things, like trips to Disney World, and things like that. It's become incredibly competitive, and it's tough. It's really hard." Money shouldn't matter in arranging interviews, but occasionally it does.

Worse, some newer organizations, ones without deep-seated roots and traditions, are now simply paying for information outright. "Now it's not just the CBSs, the NBCs, the ABCs, and CNNs out there. There's the TMZs, who admit they give people money for tips and pay for pictures and things like that," laments Mitchell. "So a young journalist just has to stay focused and realize unless you're in that world, you don't need to pay someone to give you a story. Because once you pay someone, you don't know what you're getting. People will say anything for money."

Most media organizations also have strict rules about the gifts their workers can accept. The point there is, of course, to make sure that people cannot buy positive press coverage. Beth worked in Russia, where some rich businessmen offered incredibly enticing gifts to journalists, hoping for good coverage in return. We're talking diamonds, gold watches, and even cash. But when you're faced with that kind of offer, you have to ask yourself if the gift is worth giving up your whole career, because that's what can happen if you get caught. At most news organizations, reporters can take a gift of nominal value, such as a lunch, a cup of coffee, or a pen. The point is not to make you turn down a soda if you're in someone's office doing an interview and you get thirsty. The point is to make sure that good coverage cannot be purchased. And a last word of advice: never try to resell any of the promotional materials that are routinely given to news organizations by people seeking coverage, such as DVDs of upcoming movies or new books, on sites like eBay. Such items are ethically not to be used for profit.

What matters is that you are doing what you think is right based on the standards which you hold.

—WALTER ANNENBERG, publishing magnate and diplomat

Ethical Dilemmas of the Internet Age

Because anyone can post just about anything on the Internet, the potential for unethical behavior is far greater on the Net than it is in print or broadcast. If you have a fight with your girlfriend, you're probably not going to get something bad written about her in the newspaper—but you can vent on the Web anytime you like. The Internet also poses some interesting challenges to privacy. A Facebook or MySpace account may be only for your friends, in principle—but when news happens to someone, journalists race to that person's social networking pages for information. Journalists may even set up a Web page as a way to find people to interview for a story. The Internet has also led to ethical issues over who can be considered a journalist. Many bloggers have had trouble securing press credentials because government officials have not considered them "real" journalists.

Then there is *sock puppeting*, where an author of an article may pretend to be someone else when giving feedback. If someone else writes "Great article!" about your piece, that is good. When you pretend to be a reader and write "Great article!" about something you wrote yourself, that is completely unethical. And believe it or not, reporters have been caught doing just that, and disciplined. One reporter at the *Los Angeles Times* lost his column for sock-puppeting himself.

Another problem in the computer era is that it is very easy to digitally alter photographs. Software such as Adobe Photoshop is easy to use and produces incredibly high-quality work. Photographers and photo editors use it all the time to improve the quality of photographs—to crop scenes, enrich colors, remove blemishes, and improve lighting, for example—but it can be a thin line between improving and changing a photo. Several photographers have been caught manipulating their photos to an unacceptable degree, making a fundamental change in the way a scene looked. During the Israeli-Lebanese conflict of 2006, Reuters had to pull the photos taken by a freelance photographer after an inquisitive blogger exposed that the photographer had altered some of the photos to exaggerate the damage in Lebanon made by Israeli airstrikes. Interestingly, as the technology to alter photographs has become more advanced, so has the technology that uncovers altered photos. There are now high-tech programs that can detect, for example, whether portions of a large crowd have been duplicated in a photo to make the number of people appear larger.

ETHICAL CONCERNS IN BROADCASTING. There are also specific ethical concerns that affect only broadcasting. Most television companies have rules against *staging*, which involves making events happen or getting someone to do something for the cameras. "Let's say you are at a hospital, and they want to show you a new technique but there is no patient. You can't pretend someone is a patient," says Mason. "What you can do is say that a hospital employee demonstrated how this new device works. As long as you are open about it, as long as you tell people what is happening, that's fine." In fact, it's almost impossible to shoot television news without having people do something just so you can film it. The point is not to alter the news in doing so. If you ask someone to walk a bit so you can get a setup shot of him or her, that's okay. But asking a group of people to start to protest when they are just standing around is not. And the way you edit must not misrepresent what people have said. "You can shorten sound," says Mason. "You can edit out large chunks as long as you don't change the sense of what someone is saying." There are also *decency* concerns on television. Stations need a license from the government to broadcast, and the same government agency that issues licenses, the Federal Communications Commission, also monitors complaints about indecency.

Television also has to consider *copyright*. You cannot just use pictures that belong to someone else. You can usually use only video that you have shot yourself or have purchased. There is one exception, something called *fair use*—meaning that you can show a very small bit of material that belongs to someone else if there is a news-related reason to do so. For example, when a film star dies, television stations will show some very short clips from his or her films, claiming fair use because of the newsworthiness of the story. Mason remembers a morning news producer who used some Discovery Channel animations without buying the rights to them. Of course, the Discovery Channel noticed, its lawyer called, and at that point, since the pictures had already been used, there was little that CBS News could do except pay a hefty fee or be sued. Needless to say, Mason was not happy with the producer. Rights cost money, and they can be painfully time-consuming to clear, all of which gives broadcast journalists the incentive to try to steal pictures. But if you get caught, and getting caught is very likely, it can cost a lot more in the long run.

The First Amendment has the same role in my life as a citizen and a writer as the sun has in our ecosystem.

—MICHAEL CHABON, author

The Legal Underpinning of Journalism

The U.S. Constitution did not explicitly guarantee free speech when it was written in 1787. The Bill of Rights only came along four years later. The *First Amendment* to the Constitution is the one that is most relevant to journalism: "Congress shall make no law respecting an establishment of religion, or prohibiting the free exercise thereof; or abridging the freedom of speech, or of the press; or the right of the people peaceably to assemble, and to petition the Government for a redress of grievances."

Media law, like all of American jurisprudence, is based on

precedent and analogy. Justices consider earlier cases with similar facts and issues when trying to reach a decision on a new case. Once a decision is made in a case, the principles behind it are applied to subsequent cases until a new case comes along that causes the court to change its mind, the principles are rebutted by a higher court, or the precedent is overruled by statute or amendment. The chief justice of the Supreme Court, John Roberts, tries to explain the work of our court system by comparing judges to umpires. "Umpires don't make the rules. They apply them," Roberts says. "The role of an umpire and a judge is critical. They make sure everybody plays by the rules. But it is a limited role." In fact, that may be oversimplifying, according to media law expert Arthur Hayes, Beth's colleague at Fordham. The judges on the trial level, Hayes says, are like the umpires that Roberts describes. "They apply the rules, for example, that define the strike zone, and decide whether the pitcher threw a ball or strike," he explains. "Precedent binds them; they are not allowed to redefine the strike zone." But courts on the highest levels—supreme courts or courts of appeals—have more latitude to deviate from precedent. "They are more like the commissioner of baseball," as Hayes puts it. "They say what the law is in their jurisdiction." Using the baseball analogy, the Supreme Court "can change the height and width of the strike zone," as Hayes puts it.

There are entire books on media law, and reading one before you start to work professionally is a fine idea for any young journalist. There are also some very good handbooks and guides meant specifically to give reporters the legal tools they need to do their jobs, including some free ones, as on the website of the Reporters Committee for Freedom of the Press. (See Reporters' Toolbox for details.) But here we'll give you the basics every journalist should know. We will mention a few

U.S. Supreme Court cases here, not to turn you into lawyers, but because they're so central to media law that you should know something about them. If someone mentions the *Sullivan* case, for instance, your eyes should reflect understanding, not ignorance.

LIBEL. Libel is written defamation, whereas slander is spoken defamation. Both mean that a false statement of facts has damaged someone's reputation; as a result, others shun or think less of that person. The statement must do more than annoy an individual or hurt a person's feelings.

In most countries around the world, if someone sues for libel, the onus is on the reporter to prove that what he or she wrote is the truth. Think about that for a moment. You may have gotten some information from four very reliable, independent sources that some official committed a crime. Let's say you print it, and the official sues. In most other nations, you would need to prove that the crime was committed, and just submitting the testimony of your sources wouldn't protect you from the libel charge. Here in the United States, we have a different standard—one that allows journalists to print information that they believe to be true, and to avoid punishment for many honest mistakes. The law says that when dealing with public figures—most government officials and celebrities—journalists can only be found liable for damages when the plaintiff proves *actual malice*, meaning he or she shows with convincing clarity that the reporter recklessly disregarded the truth, knew that the statement was false, or held serious doubts about its truth. This standard gives American journalists leeway, making them better able to investigate the acts of government officials and other public figures. "One of the things we are hugely blessed with in this country is the right to get it wrong," says Eve Burton, general counsel for the Hearst Corporation. But be aware that there is disagreement among the lower courts about whether an investigative reporter's motive to write a hard-hitting piece on an individual is evidence of "actual malice," and the U.S. Supreme Court has yet to settle the matter.

The central case of libel law, *New York Times v. Sullivan*, stemmed from the civil rights movement. In 1960, L. B. Sullivan, a commissioner of the city of Montgomery, Alabama, argued that he was defamed by a full-page ad in the *Times*. (Yes, publications are responsible for what appears in their advertisements as well as in articles.) The ad was about the nonviolent protests for equal rights being waged by black Americans in the South. Sullivan argued that the ad criticized the Montgomery police, which he supervised, thereby defaming him, even though it did not mention him by name. An Alabama court ruled in Sullivan's favor and awarded him $500,000—a huge amount of money at the time. The paper appealed, and the case ended up in the Supreme Court. The justices who decided the case in 1964 ruled that an honest mistake made when investigating the work of public figures was not libelous. The court found that in order to win a libel case, a government official must prove that a journalist or organization acted with actual malice. "We consider this case against the background of a profound national commitment to the principle that debate on public issues should be uninhibited, robust, and wide-open, and that it may well include vehement, caustic, and sometimes unpleasantly sharp attacks on government and public officials," said the opinion. You can find a gripping account of the whole *Sullivan* case in the book by the superb *New York Times* reporter and legal scholar Anthony Lewis, *Make No Law: The Sullivan Case and the First Amendment*.

New York Times v. Sullivan remains the basis of libel law today. Later cases extended the "actual malice" standard from government officials to public figures, who may not be elected but who still come to prominence, such as a celebrity or someone who leads a cause. Later cases clarified that if someone is not a public figure or a government official, to win a libel suit he or she merely needs to show *negligence*—failure to use due care.

If you're a reporter who gets sued for libel, you will be questioned by the other side, and they will probably ask for your notes, computer files, phone records, and anything else that will help them determine how you got your information and—if a public figure or government official is involved—whether you acted with reckless disregard for the truth or knowing falsity. If you used anonymous sources, you'll be pressed hard to reveal their names. That's why Eve Burton says she always pushes Hearst reporters to get everything they can on the record, or to get documents to back up what is being said by anonymous sources.

There's only one nearly foolproof way of avoiding a libel suit: get your story right. Burton says that she has defended at least 350 libel suits in her legal career, and in every single case the journalist got the story wrong. "You rarely get a litigation if something is entirely accurate," she explains. "Truth is a defense. People, even if they don't like what you've written, if what you've written is correct, they don't sue you." That said, none of the journalists Burton defended lost their job simply because they had caused a libel suit.

But if someone brings a libel suit against you, your reputation suffers—even if you win. That's something Mike knows all too well. As we mentioned earlier, in 1982 Mike was sued by former U.S. Army general William Westmoreland over an episode of *CBS Reports* entitled "The Uncounted Enemy." The program alleged that during the Vietnam War, the U.S. government systematically and deliberately undercounted the number of North Vietnamese soldiers fighting against U.S. and South Vietnamese forces. The point was to make it appear that the United States was winning the Vietnam War and to keep the fighting going by making the enemy seem weaker than it was. Westmoreland, the chief U.S. general in South Vietnam from 1964 to 1968, was an integral part of the story. "Westy and Lyndon Johnson lied to the American people about the enemy out there, because they knew damn well that if the public began to understand how many enemy were in fact out there in North Vietnam, all support for the war would be gone," Mike explains. In the documentary, Westmoreland denied all of the charges, but the program still presented a damning portrait.

Westmoreland sued for libel, seeking $120 million in damages, spurred on by a report in *TV Guide* magazine that said that Mike's report was put together in a way that violated the network's standards. The general named CBS News and four individuals as defendants, including Mike. (As a government official, Westmoreland had to prove with convincing clarity that the accusations were made with reckless falsity.) The proceedings dragged on for nearly three years. Mike felt sure he had reported the facts right and that they'd win the suit. That feeling was backed up by CBS News' own internal investigation, which found that while the "The Uncounted Enemy" was made in a flawed manner, the central arguments made by the documentary all appeared to be true.

The court process was unpleasant for all involved, but particularly for Mike, who felt that the reputation he had built over several decades of work was being unfairly put on trial.

"When he sued us for libel, we went to court and I had to sit in that courtroom, day after day, while Westy's lawyers put people on the stand who I think unfairly portrayed our story," Mike remembers. Yet Mike and the CBS team held on, believing that they would be found exonerated. Abruptly, just two days before Mike was scheduled to take the stand, Westmoreland withdrew his suit. In the end, CBS issued a statement saying that it "never intended to assert . . . General Westmoreland was unpatriotic or disloyal in performing his duties as he saw them." Both sides paid their own legal fees, and Westmoreland won no money in the end.

Still, the trial sent Mike into a deep depression, which lasted for months afterward. (See his 2005 book *Between You and Me* for an extensive discussion of the Westmoreland case and the depression that followed it.) Yet despite the personal cost, looking back at the Westmoreland trial more than twenty-five years later, Mike sees why "The Uncounted Enemy" was important. "From time to time, your government would lie to you. And the government was consistently lying to the American people back then. They did not want to tell the truth," Mike explains. "This, you began to understand, was the power of the press," he says. "It told the truth. It spoke the truth to power."

Almost any kind of journalistic work that exposes government wrongdoing also puts the journalist who does it in a delicate and often stressful position. But we journalists in the United States are lucky that the consequences for us are usually limited only to stress. In many other countries, journalists are jailed, tortured, or killed for digging into corruption or government malfeasance. Check out the work of the Committee to Protect Journalists, which documents attacks against journalists around the world, and you'll see what we mean.

And speaking of other countries, here's a concept that you should know: *libel tourism*. Some people who believe they have been libeled by American writers are now trying to sue in other countries where the libel laws offer less protection to journalists. It's already happened to American book authors whose works, while not published in Great Britain, can be ordered there, in effect creating jurisdiction. Britain's libel laws are notoriously slanted in favor of plaintiffs. And there's a possibility that libel tourism is going to spread. Libel is generally seen as happening wherever an article is read, meaning that articles on the Internet potentially may be open to libel prosecution anywhere in the world. That would erode the protection American journalists have been given by our courts. This worries some members of Congress, who are trying to draft a federal law to outlaw libel tourism. The state of New York already passed a law to protect New York authors and publishers. This area of the law is evolving and bears watching.

The greatest dangers to liberty lurk in the insidious encroachment by men of zeal, well meaning but without understanding.

—LOUIS D. BRANDEIS, Supreme Court Justice

There are a few more areas of the law that every journalist should understand.

PRIOR RESTRAINT. We briefly touched upon blocking publication of sensitive materials when we discussed the ethics of national security. More generally, the legal issue is called *prior restraint*. Prior restraint is the government's ability to stop a news organization from publishing or broadcasting something, or preventing the continuation of publication. Journalists generally believe it is better for the government to let them do what they like and then punish them later if they have broken the law. In legalese, that's called *subsequent punishment*. But what if national security is at stake? Most government officials would try to stop the publication of something that they thought would adversely damage American interests. Luckily for the press, journalists can take the government to court in such cases, where judges have been reluctant to block publication. That's because the U.S. Supreme Court has said that prior restraint is presumptively unconstitutional.

The precedent-setting case in the area of prior restraint is from 1931, *Near v. Minnesota*. The case is the subject of a delightful book by the late CBS News producer and journalism professor Fred W. Friendly, *Minnesota Rag*—a work well worth your time if you're interested in media law or media history. Jay M. Near started publishing a newspaper called the *Saturday Press* in 1927 in Minneapolis. It was sensational, anti-Semetic, anti-Catholic, racist, and, as Friendly put it, a rag. And it made plenty of enemies by criticizing local officials. A county judge ordered the paper closed for creating a public nuisance, and the Minnesota Supreme Court upheld the order, saying in effect that the First Amendment right to freedom of speech didn't apply to upstarts such as the *Saturday Press*. The case went all the way to the U.S. Supreme Court, where the justices took the view that prior restraint was unconstitutional in all but a few very limited circumstances—and that this wasn't one of them. "The fact that the liberty of the press may be abused by miscreant purveyors of scandal does not make any the less necessary the immunity of the press from previous restraint in dealing with official misconduct," said the decision.

"Even a more serious public evil would be caused by authority to prevent publication."

The courts revisited the idea of prior restraint many years later, in 1971, when the *New York Times* and three other newspapers published parts of the Pentagon Papers. The Supreme Court case, *New York Times Company v. United States*, is fascinating for a few reasons. First of all, instead of dragging on for months like most Supreme Court cases, this one took only about a week from start to finish. Also, it is one of the rare cases where each of the nine Supreme Court justices wrote a separate opinion—each agreeing that the Pentagon Papers should be printed immediately, but disagreeing on the reasons why. Thanks to the court's strong stand in these cases and others, prior restraint in the United States is extremely rare. (Requiring broadcasters to obtain a government license, however, is one major exception.) The restraint in the media that we generally see is done voluntarily, as in the case of *New York Times* reporter David Rohde's kidnapping.

CENSORSHIP. Censorship is a large and rather complicated part of American media law, regulated by both the federal government and states. Things judged *obscene*, such as certain kinds of pornography, can and have been banned—and breaking obscenity laws can lead to fines and arrest. The Supreme Court set the standard for what can be considered obscene in the case *Miller v. California* in 1973: "(a) whether the average person applying contemporary community standards would find that the work, taken as a whole, appeals to a prurient interest; (b) whether the work depicts or describes, in a patently offensive way, sexual conduct specifically defined by the applicable state law; and (c) whether the work, taken as a whole, lacks serious literary, artistic, political, or scientific value." As you can see, those definitions are open to interpretation, which is why people often complain about obscenity law. "The F.C.C.'s indecency policy is hopelessly vague," writes the *New York Times*. "Broadcasters have no way of knowing in advance what sort of content will upset the F.C.C.'s indecency policy." Even a Supreme Court justice once said that he couldn't define *pornography* but he knew it when he saw it.

The Federal Communications Commission regulates obscenity on television and radio, using the same Supreme Court standard as for print. That means that nothing obscene should ever appear on any television or radio station. The FCC also makes and monitors stricter rules regarding indecency and profanity—but only for free-to-air television and radio, not cable, satellite, or Internet broadcasting. That's one of the reasons you can get away with a lot more nudity and cursing on cable shows than you can on broadcast television. What does the FCC consider *indecent*? Its definition is written in dense, legalistic language: "Material is indecent if, in context, it depicts or describes sexual or excretory organs or activities in terms patently offensive as measured by contemporary community standards for the broadcast medium," says the commission. "In each case, the FCC must determine whether the material describes or depicts sexual or excretory organs or activities and, if so, whether the material is 'patently offensive.'" The FCC says indecent material should not be aired between the hours of 6:00 a.m. and 10:00 p.m., when children are likely to be watching. And what does the commission describe as *profanity*? "'Profane language' includes those words that are so highly offensive that their mere utterance in the context presented may, in legal terms, amount to a 'nuisance,'" says the agency. The FCC has warned broadcasters that the *F*-word and other curses are generally profane and cannot be broadcast between 6:00 a.m. and 10:00 p.m. Broadcasters try to adhere to that, but occasionally someone will blurt out a curse word during a live broadcast during those hours—which can lead to heavy fines. There have been plenty of high-profile cases about these kinds of *fleeting expletives* lately—and many free speech advocates say this part of the law needs updating, since there's little harm done nowadays by the occasional four-letter word on television.

Censorship on the Internet is far more complex than in print or broadcast. The U.S. government and courts are still grappling with how to extend obscenity laws to the Internet. Free speech advocates such as the American Civil Liberties Union (ACLU) have been active in trying to keep the U.S. Internet free of government controls. The ACLU and other groups are also trying to keep the Web "Net neutral," meaning free of corporate controls. The ACLU doesn't want Internet service providers to determine which sites users can see and which they can't, unlike the way cable television providers operate. For example, they don't want Internet service providers to block access to sites that complain about that ISP's service or to block sites such as PayPal because the ISP owns part of another online payment service.

SHIELD LAWS. Journalists sometimes make a promise of anonymity to their sources, as a way to get information the interviewee could not give them any other way. But in some cases, the government or a court may have a reason to want to know the name of that confidential source, usually because the source appears to be involved in or know about a crime. Journalists are regularly ordered to court to testify, or asked to appear before grand juries—panels that try to determine whether to formally charge someone with a crime. Some journalists go when called and give up the names of their sources, but others do not, arguing that they made a promise of confidentiality that they cannot break. Many journalists have gone to jail, some for months, rather than reveal the names of the sources to whom they promised anonymity. Many reporters resent the idea that they need to appear before juries or grand juries like anyone else, although the courts have generally held that journalists aren't above the law in this regard.

This has been a particularly interesting area of the law during recent years, because President George W. Bush's administration dramatically ramped up the number of journalists dragged into court. Eve Burton says that at Hearst—which owns newspapers, magazines, and television stations—the number of reporters subpoenaed rose from just a handful each year to between 125 and 175 annually. She says the Bush administration apparently thought journalists provided an easy way to get high-quality information, using logic like this: "Who would you rather have information from, a convicted felon in a jailhouse interview or the local reporter, who's probably pretty smart in covering something? And everyone decided that the best information in the country was out there, and it was gathered by young reporters and investigative reporters, and let's haul 'em all in," Burton explains. "And you really saw this incredible uptick of first-stop shopping as opposed to last-stop shopping of the press." That's one of the reasons why there have been fresh efforts to pass a federal shield law, which would define reporters' rights when it comes to confidential sources.

Currently, more than half of the states have *shield laws* that give some rights to reporters and allow them to shield their sources from being identified. But there has never been a federal shield law, and that has effectively limited the rights of journalists. "If you cover a drug story, and the drug case gets prosecuted in federal court, right now you have no protection to protect confidential sources," explains Burton. "But if the very same case with the very same facts is prosecuted in the state courts, you have an absolute right to protect your sources. It's virtually impossible to exercise your state right if you don't have an equivalent federal right." The Obama administration, unlike its predecessor, is in favor of a federal shield law, and as we were writing this book, a bill establishing one was making its way through Congress.

TRESPASS. *Trespass* means to be on private property without permission, or on public property that is closed to the public without authorization. Some well-known cases involving trespassing were ones in which journalists misrepresented themselves to get access to a place. The most infamous of these is called the Food Lion case. In 1992, ABC News received information that the Food Lion chain of supermarkets was selling food past its expiration date—and trying to cover it up. The information alleged that Food Lion was bleaching meat to remove discoloration, blending expired and fresh meat together, and changing the expiration dates on food packages. Two ABC News producers, both women, lied about their identities and background and were hired at Food Lion—one in North Carolina and one in South Carolina. During two weeks, the two women secretly shot about forty-five hours of hidden-camera footage, showing that the charges against the chain were true. The video became the basis for an episode of the newsmagazine *Primetime Live*. Food Lion sued ABC News and the show's producers, not for libel (since the story was true) but for other crimes including trespass, fraud, and unfair trade practices. A lower court found ABC News guilty on most charges and ordered it to pay more than $5 million in damages to Food Lion. But on appeal, the journalists were found guilty of only trespass and breach of duty, and instead of $5 million, they were ordered to pay just $2 in damages to the supermarket chain. But even as they reduced the judgment, the justices said that journalists are not immune from the law.

That being said, the courts have often been understanding when reporters broke the law to show that something posed a threat to public safety or democracy. A reporter who voted five times in Idaho to show how easy it was to break election laws had his case dismissed by a judge, as did a TV crew that got into restricted areas at New York's Kennedy Airport to illustrate security lapses. So what if you need to sneak in somewhere for an investigation or misrepresent yourself to get information you need? How do you balance the public's right to hear an important story with the potential legal ramifications of getting that story? That's where your editor usually comes in. Most news organizations have rules about when, if ever, trespassing or misrepresentation might be allowed.

Taste cannot be controlled by law.

—THOMAS JEFFERSON, U.S. president

If You Get into Trouble

These are tricky issues. It's easy to advise that whenever someone asks you to do something that is potentially unethical or illegal, you should resist. And knowing the basics we've covered above will certainly help protect you in that respect.

But the truth is, nearly every journalist we know has made some kind of decision he or she later regretted.

The good news is, if you make a mistake that could get you sued, you can probably count on your organization to try to wiggle out of the situation without heading to court. Linda Mason says that CBS News almost always tries to offer someone with a valid complaint a way to resolve it without going to court. "We see if there is a way to placate them, sometimes putting a note on the Web next to the article or the piece, editor's note, correction, expansion—that does it," she says. "The last thing that we want to do is get to an impasse. So very often when you get complaints, you have to take them seriously, address them immediately, and see if there is a way to work out an agreement in the early stage. The worst thing you can do is throw it away and say they are crazy, because then it reaches the suit stage—and that is a very expensive proposition, even if you end up being right and winning."

Often, retractions, corrections, and apologies not only are good ways to try to head off legal actions but are just the right thing to do. Burton says that when she worked at the New York *Daily News* a few years ago, she introduced a template that the paper could use to print an apology when it got something wrong. "We didn't just fix the error. We apologized for the error," she explains. "When I got there it used to be 'The *Daily News* regrets that you feel bad about the error.' Now it's 'The *Daily News* regrets the error.' It's very important to say sorry." Many newspapers also have what's called an ombudsman, who reviews and evaluates the publication's work. Although the ombudsman is employed by the paper, he or she is usually given a mandate to criticize as necessary to improve the publication, and is often someone to whom readers and viewers can turn with complaints.

And if you do make a mistake that actually causes a lawsuit for your organization, it's not necessarily a career-ending move. Mike's career is proof of that. Of course, it's undesirable for a journalist to get into legal trouble—or ethical trouble, for that matter—but some mistakes are understandable, and part of the learning process. "It's other people's responsibility as well—because you are young, they should have been overseeing what you are doing," Mason points out. Even Mason had her own brushes with legal issues in her early days at CBS. "I, as a young producer, did a piece for the *Evening News*—it was dealing with some product that was dangerous, some ingredient in a product, so I went out and bought a bunch of the product and arranged them on a desk" for a shot, she remembers. Later, while she was on vacation, Mason was sent a note that one of the products they had shown on the news did not in fact have the dangerous ingredient in it. "I thought I'd die," she recalls. "We made a correction and everything was okay. But you have got to be very, very careful."

7

THE FUTURE: ADVICE FOR THE NEXT GENERATION OF JOURNALISTS

I really believe good journalism is good business.

—CHRISTIANE AMANPOUR, journalist and author

When Beth tells her students that she wrote her college papers on a typewriter and researched them using books in the library, they look at her with quizzical expressions. No computers? No Internet? And of course when Mike graduated from college in 1939, television and computers were still being developed, and the cutting-edge way to get breaking news was on the radio. Young people nowadays are so technologically advanced that they can hardly imagine life without the Internet or wireless technology.

Certainly, technology has changed enormously during our lifetimes, and it is still evolving. A main challenge for journalists today lies in figuring out how to embrace the latest technological advances while remaining true to the traditions of fine journalism. That's what we'll be discussing in this last chapter.

The Current Landscape

There's some fantastic journalism being produced right now—stories that shed new light on crucially important issues. But, frankly, there's also a lot of crap. As Lin Garlick puts it, news has become "lighter and tighter." Sometimes as we watch television or read some of the newspapers and magazines that cross our paths, we get riled up because the coverage is so bad—either it's shallow, it's sensational, or it's trivial.

We love the idea of news coverage being available twenty-four hours a day, but we're not crazy about the increasing focus on opinion, gossip, and scandal that we see nowadays. "A lot of it is drivel and crap," says Mike. "It becomes a lot of tabloid and self-conscious controversy, a lot of manufactured controversy. What used to pass for news, what used to be news on the networks, really doesn't exist in the way that it used to." He feels that most news today is a far cry from what he and his colleagues produced back in the heyday of CBS News in the 1960s and '70s. "We were at the top, always, always because the audience respected us. Then cable came, and what has happened to news as far as I'm concerned is that it's yammer, yammer, yammer. It's infotainment," Mike explains. "It used to be a race to the top. To a certain degree, news today is a race to the bottom."

That race to the bottom is exacerbated by budget cuts, which too often lead journalists to try to report a story without being there. Small staffs mean that reporters may lack the expertise to do a story right but have to do it anyway. Beth saw one such story as she was finishing this book about Russian prime minister Vladimir Putin, and how he had frequently been appearing shirtless. To the average viewer, the story seemed fine. But Beth, who knew something about Russia and

Putin, found it to be overly simplistic, about six years too late, and missing nearly all the important points. Still, it's hard to fault the reporter, who didn't live in Russia, had hardly ever been to Russia, and couldn't be expected to produce high-quality journalism about Russia. The problem is the current system of journalism, which stresses quantity over quality, ratings and ad revenue over content.

News has always been a business, but the financial demands on journalism were far less imposing years ago. One of the reasons why CBS News was for decades the premier broadcast news company is that the founder of CBS, William S. Paley, believed CBS News should serve the public and not worry about making money. Marvin Kalb remembers being at a dinner with Paley in 1962 where the founder of CBS laid out his plans for the news division for the following year. They were ambitious plans, and one correspondent asked how Paley would pay for them. "And Paley answered—and this is almost a direct quote—'You guys cover the news. I've got Jack Benny to make money for me,'" Kalb recalls. "He knew that news was losing money, but he also knew that he could make money from the entertainment aspects of the CBS business. He didn't expect news to make money then, so he would fill up the pot and give us whatever we needed. That meant spending whatever money you had to spend in order to get the story." Other former CBS News staffers remember that during the 1960s and '70s, they weren't allowed to see the ratings. Managers didn't want the ratings hung up in the newsroom, and didn't want anyone except the top executives to even think about them. That, too, is a far cry from today.

But in the early 1970s, all that began to change. After *60 Minutes* started to make huge amounts of money, media managers figured out that news could be a highly profitable product.

In the 1970s and '80s, corporations started to buy up media businesses, many of which had been family-owned, tilting the whole meaning of journalism toward making money. "Once that happened, everything flowed from it, because if a news operation could make money it had to live by the standards of a regular business," explains Kalb. "Up to that point, we were a treasured, cherished asset of the industry—but not a business component. Once we became this component, the standards and the ethics changed." By the 1990s, the profits were flowing into news businesses, but at an unsustainably high rate. Some newspapers, for instance, were making pretax profits of about 30 percent—several times what might be considered a healthy profit for a manufacturer or retail store chain.

All this means that nowadays, the bottom line at journalistic organizations too often is money, not serving the public good. If you're a reporter pitching a story, editors' first question is usually "How much will the story cost?" rather than "Is it worth doing?" And that's not usually by the editors' choice—it's just reality. Thank goodness, there are some news organizations and some crusading reporters that are still driven by the public interest. But as we write this book, they've been taking a beating, as the poor economy has applied a death grip to many news outlets. Reporters have been fired in droves, and publications are folding right and left. For the very first time, a major American city may soon find itself without a daily newspaper. And all the cutbacks create a vicious circle. Smaller staffs usually have to cut back on enterprise reporting—the original, creative reporting that usually involves analysis or investigation. It's that kind of original reporting that pulls in an audience. The lack of enterprise reporting leads to a smaller audience, which means more reporters have to be fired, and so on, and so on.

The profit motive doesn't affect just enterprise reporting. Take the change of anchors at our beloved CBS News, for example. When Katie Couric was brought in to replace Dan Rather in 2006 (after a short and very successful interim anchorship by Bob Schieffer), management didn't seem to really be looking for the best journalist for the job. The point seemed to be to hire whoever would bring in the most new viewers. Mike puts it bluntly: as much as he likes Couric as a person, CBS News hired her "because she was perky" and because they thought a female anchor would be appealing. And who brought in Couric? Mike says the decision was made by Leslie Moonves, the president of CBS—not the president of CBS News, but president of the whole CBS network. "He wasn't the news director. He is the guy that turned CBS Entertainment around," explains Mike. According to the *New York Times*, Moonves invited entertainment executives from other parts of the CBS corporate family to join top CBS News staff in discussions over the anchor. Moonves said publicly during the search that he didn't want "the voice-of-God, single-anchor" format to continue. "One of the things we're looking at is having something that is younger, more relevant," he said, "as opposed to that guy preaching from the mountaintop about what we should and should not watch." And that's exactly what he's tried to do with Couric. "He brought her in because he thought he was going to get a younger, more with-it audience," Mike says. "I have talked to him about it. Because he had been successful with entertainment and turning CBS around on entertainment shows, he said that if he had the opportunity to revamp news, he would somehow lure viewers. He wanted to keep the old viewers and add the new."

Good thinking, perhaps, except it hasn't worked out as well as the CBS executives had hoped. *The CBS Evening News with Katie Couric* is still third in the ratings at 6:30 p.m.—despite some excellent work, such as Couric's interview with the 2008 Republican vice presidential candidate, Sarah Palin. But Couric's audience hasn't gotten younger. In fact, studies show that the average age of the *CBS Evening News* viewer has actually gone *up* since Couric took over, to just over sixty-one.

CBS and the other broadcast networks have finally figured out that reaching that coveted young audience is just not going to happen at 6:30 at night, when few people are at home. If they're going to get young viewers, they're going to get them on the Internet. So the broadcast networks, and the cable networks, too, for that matter, are putting more and more resources into their websites. In addition to offering both live and on-demand broadcasts on the Web, the networks are using their websites to cover more raw news, including speeches, congressional hearings, and press conferences. They're also putting a lot of unique content on the Web, from webcasts to complete interview outtakes. Newspapers and magazines are following suit by beefing up their websites and adding new features such as videos and interactive graphics.

In terms of attracting that younger audience, not only is this a smart way to go, it's the only way to go. This is the content and coverage that the Web-savvy generation has come to expect from news organizations. There's just one problem: nobody's figured out how to make online coverage as profitable as print or TV. It used to be that news websites thought they could build a following and then live off the ads companies would buy to reach that audience. But that hasn't turned out to be the case, because online advertising still brings in just a fraction of what print ads and commercials do. That's led many media organizations to consider charging for access to their websites. But when websites start to charge, most people just go elsewhere. Take the well-regarded British paper the *Financial Times*, for example. FT.com had more than 1 million registered users in 2001, when it started charging for some online content. After the tollbooth went into effect, the number of registered users dropped to around 50,000 the first year before climbing back up to about 100,000 in 2009. But that's a small fraction of the number of people who used to use the site. Both the *New York Times* and *Los Angeles Times* also tried charging readers for some content, and both ended up changing their schemes.

Add into that bleak scenario the fact that traditional advertising revenues have fallen at most media organizations. At newspapers, for instance, estimates are that overall ad revenue fell by about 25 percent from 2006 to 2008. Broadcast television ad revenues were down by an estimated 12 percent in the first half of 2009 alone.

So if websites stay free and the current trends of falling income continue, some news organizations will end up going broke. And if organizations start charging for content as a way to supplement advertising, few people will be willing to pay, so the news organization will also be in danger of going bust. That's the current conundrum.

It's pretty clear that journalism needs a new business model to break the existing vicious circle, and a lot of people who are a lot smarter than us are working on solutions. "I think we'll figure this out," says Bill Keller, executive editor of the *New York Times*. "We're examining every possible permutation of business models." But the bottom line is that people are going to have to pay in some way for things that they have been able to get for free. That's not a big deal to people older than about forty, who were used to paying for a newspaper and so probably won't feel too bad about paying for news content now.

But for those in the younger generations, it's going to be a huge change—and one they're probably not going to be very happy to make. If you've only ever read things for free online, it's going to be strange to have to start paying, and polls show few people are willing to pay outright for online news. And we're deeply worried about what's going to happen when these younger consumers are asked to pay for news content, given how little news most of them consume now while it's free. Journalism will stay alive only if more young people today understand just how important it is that they stay well informed, and become devoted consumers of the news.

I have now one ambition: to retire before it becomes essential to tweet.

—REPRESENTATIVE BARNEY FRANK (D-Mass.)

The Future of Journalism

So where is journalism going? Here's where we think we're headed in the next few years, given the trends and technological advances that continue to shape journalism.

THE VAST MAJORITY OF PRINT PUBLICATIONS WILL NO LONGER PRINT HARD COPIES. They will be Internet-only publications, and readers will fund them through direct or indirect payments. That will be a tough change for the older generation, but as those people pass on, people who came of age in the Internet era will think it's completely normal for most newspapers and magazines to exist only online. We think this change will actually take longer than some people think, but it is inevitable. But the form may not matter as long as the content is still strong. "I don't think it ultimately matters whether newspapers survive or not," says Marcus Brauchli, top editor of the *Washington Post*. "What matters is that journalism survives, that it remains independent, that it holds the state and the powerful accountable. What matters is that journalism continues to serve society by ensuring that our citizens, policy makers, friends, and rivals have access to deep, accurate, and comprehensive information about our communities, our nation, and the world."

OTHER MEDIA WILL CHANGE, TOO. "I have two young daughters and I can't imagine that they'll be listening to radio frequencies when they grow up," says Robert Smith of National Public Radio. "Radio, as in FM and AM, will become less relevant. But audio will live on. Whether through the Internet, iPod, cell phone, or whatever's next, audio reporting will be there. First of all, there will always be times when you can't look at something: while driving, jogging, or doing the dishes. Audio is still perfect for those times. And more than convenience, I think we all love to be told a story. The human voice won't go out of style, and organizations like NPR who know how to bring those voices into our lives won't go away." Journalists and news organizations, though, will be challenged to find ways to use technology not just to do things faster and more quickly, but to deepen understanding.

PEOPLE WILL WANT NEWS ON DEMAND. Broadcasters will have to adapt and make sure that viewers can access news broadcasts anytime, in ways that are convenient for them. People might wait for a new episode of *60 Minutes* to come out on Sunday nights, but once the episode is out, they will want an easy way to find and watch it.

NEWS WILL BECOME MORE FOCUSED AND MORE PERSONALIZED. As resources continue to be cut, news organizations may have to limit their scope and focus their resources on doing fewer things overall. "I think we're headed toward a journalism world in which there's a bigger division between local/regional and national news," says Joshua Micah Marshall of Talking Points Memo. "The logic of a small town paper or website or even regional paper/website also independently covering national news is far weaker, in editorial and business terms." Marshall says that it's hard to think that a major metropolitan paper in a place such as Ohio will be able to cover national news at a level that will make it a more logical destination on those subjects for Ohio readers than the *New York Times*, MSNBC, the *Washington Post*, the Huffington Post, or other national media. "So I think in the national hard news and political news space we're looking at a future in which there are maybe a dozen national Web-based publications dominating that space," Marshall says. Simultaneously, niche websites and online publications will grow to reach consumers as economic limitations force general publications to cut back on their coverage of specialized topics. News consumers will also find new ways to personalize their favorite websites to provide a better online experience.

MULTITASKING WILL BE THE NORM. When we watch young people, we notice that they can do three or four things at the same time—like writing a paper while watching TV, listening to music, and talking on the phone. Our generations used to multitask, too—but today's young people are able to do more things simultaneously than ever. Multitasking like that may be normal for young people, but the downside is that each task receives less attention than it would get if only one thing were going on. Studies show people tend to absorb information more slowly if they're doing several things simultaneously. That means that journalists will be pressed to start their reports with a bang. And television news may become ambient noise unless it's compelling enough to make people focus.

TECHNOLOGY WILL CONTINUE TO DRIVE NEWS COVERAGE. We're not yet at the point where people can turn their telephone into a mobile television studio or watch every television station live on their cell phones. But those days are surely coming. People will use every technological advance to create faster, more mobile, and (we hope) better press coverage. We've already seen this with satellite dishes. It used to be that you needed a satellite dish to beam video from one side of the world to another. Now all you need is an Internet or cell phone connection and some widely available file-transfer software, and you can send high-quality video anywhere in the world. It's so much cheaper and easier to send a story this way than by satellite that TV networks are asking correspondents to use it whenever possible.

WE FACE INFORMATION OVERLOAD. With so many news outlets and blogs on the Internet, it already can be hard to know what to read or watch. And that's only going to get worse as more sites spring up, fostered by new technologies. People are going to have to figure out how to limit the amount of information sent to them via the Internet, and also how to use their Internet time more efficiently. That's one reason why there's reason to think that there is a future for high-quality media organizations. "With so many voices out there, so many blogs, everyone has a printing press, so to speak, these days," says Scott Pelley of *60 Minutes*. "I think people are going to gravitate to brands they know and brands they trust." People will want help in making sense of all the information out there. It's one thing to be able to hear a presidential address. It's quite another to have a trusted voice identifying the new initiatives being discussed and otherwise putting the speech in context.

PEOPLE WILL STILL WANT TO GO TO TRUSTED WEBSITES. People already understand that not everything on the Web is correct. That is why they trust mainstream news organizations to maintain standards of accuracy and fairness. "In this infinite ocean of information, people seek out islands of clarity," says Brauchli. "They went dependable sources. They want facts that are facts, news with context and fairness in how it is presented. This is the great power and virtue of journalism." As the Web grows, trust will become more and more of an issue.

PEOPLE WILL STILL MAKE THE NEWS. The news business will still require thousands and thousands of trained professionals to run all those trusted news organizations. "People talk about big media like it's a pejorative. But God help us if we don't have big media," says Pelley. "Big media like CBS, like the *New York Times*, like the Associated Press, have traditions and infrastructure that filter information. We are professionals, and I have editors, and my editors have editors, and the information flows through this enormous filter that's called *60 Minutes*, that's called CBS News, so that when it comes out to the public, the public can rely on the fact that numbers of professionals have examined the information for fairness and accuracy. Now, we don't always get it right. We make mistakes, and every once in a great while we make spectacular mistakes. However, when you consider the amount of information we work through, every single day, on deadline, week in and week out, the quality is extremely high."

CONTENT WILL COME FROM EVERYONE, NOT JUST FROM JOURNALISTS. There will be more and more content from regular citizens, as more and more people become Web savvy. Just look at the explosion of sites such as Twitter and YouTube and you'll see that everyone can already share information 24/7. Ordinary people are already providing the kind of eyewitness reports using their cell phones that only journalists could do even a few years ago. And that trend is going to continue as the technology becomes more sophisticated. The challenge will be to make all that user-generated content meaningful, and to make sure that the accurate information gets noticed and the bad information gets weeded out. "I fear if we require fewer journalists to do more, then they will have less time to be accurate—and if we depend more on the Wikipedias and the blogosphere, we will again be passing around misinformation over and over and over," says Robert Anderson. Market forces may turn out to be helpful in this. If people don't read certain sites, those sites may die. And if people have really good ideas, the Internet will help them develop those ideas. We find the new investigative reporting websites such as Spot.Us, where readers can chip in to fund stories, absolutely fascinating, and a great way to help create high-quality content.

RESOURCES WILL CONTINUE TO MATTER. With all the information on the Internet, people will still be looking for something new, interesting, and important. Organizations with strong original reporting will continue to stay relevant. Enterprise reporting often costs a lot of money, meaning that only the largest news organizations are likely to do really large-scale investigative projects. "My trip into Darfur that exposed the destruction of the village by the government forces—that trip probably cost a quarter of a million dollars. Some guy working in his basement as a blogger isn't going to pull that off. It's not going to happen," explains Pelley. "If you want to expose the big lies and the big injustices that are perpetrated by governments, you need to have a very strong, well-financed, and robust organization to take on that kind of thing." By spending money, news organizations will not only increase the chance of holding on to their audience but also increase their chances of fulfilling the media's all-important watchdog function.

Never take yourself too seriously. You may be interviewing the President today, but tomorrow you're covering a dog wedding.

—DREW GRIFFIN, journalist

What Does This Mean for Journalists Today?

As you've probably surmised, we think that reporting skills are paramount. Today and in the future, your ability to succeed in the news business depends on being able to come up with novel story ideas and to complete them in a professional way, living up to the standards we've laid out in these pages. But given the way the news business is going, good reporting might not be enough anymore. It takes technological savvy, too. If you can shoot a camera, put together a website, or edit audio, video, and photos, it will help make you valuable to your news organization, especially if it's a small one. "I think that's the way the industry is going. I really do," says Russ Mitchell. "I think that it's just a matter of time before they give us all cameras at the network level and say, 'Okay, here's your camera. Go out and shoot.'"

People with multifaceted journalism skills are already finding themselves in demand. "When I was at the University of Missouri a few weeks ago, that very day there was a television station in Dallas—Dallas, Texas, the eighth-largest market in the country—recruiting for a one-man-band journalist," recalls Mitchell. "Twenty-two years old—bam—and you could go right to Dallas if you know how to shoot, edit, report, put your story on the Internet, file a story for a newspaper. And that was unheard of back in the day." It's the same story in radio. "A radio reporter these days has to do a lot more. We all write Web copy, take photos, some even do video," Robert Smith says.

"We employ what we call hyphenates: writer-producer-editors," says Lin Garlick. "They not only can write the piece, they can go out and produce the elements, do the interviews, bring them back, and then they sit down and physically edit the videotape. And I think the next step is writer-producer-editor-shooters. One-man bands." That may be the cheapest way for a news organization to work, but she says it's very hard to find people who can do all those things well. And she says the hardest thing to find is someone who's a good writer. "It's almost impossible," laments Garlick. "I find I can get plenty of people who can shoot, plenty of people who can edit videotape. The dying trade is TV writing. Definitely." Garlick says that when she gives potential employees a writing test and asks them to produce a short script, only about one in fifteen people can actually do it at a level fit for broadcast. That's proof that writing well, whether for broadcast or print, helps you get attention.

The way to improve your writing is to write. Analyzing scripts or stories by writers you like is also instructive. "Find the storytellers you love and call them up," advises Smith.

"People do this to me all the time. They'll just ask: 'How did you do that?' And I can talk for hours. To this day, I'll still dissect a story from some other reporter I love and figure out what makes it tick." Reading great writers can also help. "Read good fiction—like Dickens, Cheever, Chekhov, and Raymond Carver—to figure out how to describe people and hint at character and motivation," advises reporter Anthony Ramirez. Finding a mentor or coach to help you improve your writing can also help.

HOW TO START. People often ask us what the best career path is if you want to end up at a major newspaper, magazine, or station. They want to know if it's better to start as a reporter at a small paper or station, perhaps in a small city, or to start as an assistant at a large newspaper, magazine, or network. The reality is that either one can work. "In television right now there are two broad routes," says Anderson. "One is the old tried-and-true of 'go to the smallest affiliate you need to, to do whatever it is you want to get good at, because the point is to get good at it.' If you want to be an on-camera reporter, then go to a tiny town in Texas where you can be an on-camera reporter and start getting good at what you want to be good at. The other route says, 'I can get really good in Texas, but no one in New York is ever going to know I exist. So I'll get a job ripping scripts at the morning news, and I'll impress everybody around me with how bright and hardworking I am, and I'll end up doing local stories in time in front of a camera.' They both work."

Of the people we know in this industry, the vast majority started at small organizations and worked their way up to large ones. "One of the things I always say to young journalists is start out in a smaller pond with greater responsibility. I think people who start out at networks or major newspapers and have a job as a desk assistant are wasting their time," says Chris Wallace. "If you're any good, particularly with DVDs and the Net, you'll get found, you'll get discovered, and you'll be able to move up." In the past, starting small meant going to a small-town paper or tiny affiliate, but today it may mean landing a job at some up-and-coming online news site. The principle is the same. That doesn't mean that there's no path up from the bottom of a large news organization. Linda Mason, for one, started at CBS News as a desk assistant and made it to senior vice president.

Another good way to make your work stand out is to become a specialist in some area of coverage. It can be pretty much anything—law, sports, science, the environment—but it should be something that really interests you. The great professor Joseph Campbell told students to "follow your bliss," which is advice we support wholeheartedly. You can get this expertise either by getting a graduate degree or by taking a job outside journalism. If you spend a year or two working on Capitol Hill, for instance, you'd obviously get a lot of insider knowledge that would then help you cover Congress. Christopher Chivers of the *New York Times*, who served as a Marine before turning to journalism, says his military training often helps him in his work. He cites as an example his coverage of the 2004 Beslan siege, where more than 1,200 people were taken hostage in a southern Russian school. The school was laced with bombs, several of which went off on the last day of the siege. "Knowing weapons and tactics made it much easier to understand what we were observing that day, and to sort through much of the nonsense that circulated afterward," Chivers explains. "Loopy stories and accounts of that siege and the final battle were trafficked by the government and by no small number of journalists, and I would have been more likely to echo them, as many people did, if I had not known what I do about how weapons work." Chivers, not coincidentally, won two national awards for his reporting on Beslan.

Another great idea for advancement: travel. Foreign reporting is a wonderful specialty, and your career can really flourish if you have the skills and knowledge to work in a foreign country—especially if that country is in the news. But you need to speak the language to really be of use. Beth can remember being very frustrated about how little she could do in her first year or two in Moscow because of her lack of Russian-language skills. "I worked with a tutor on my Russian for about ten years," she says. "I had to use a translator for maybe the first two years, but then my Russian got good enough to do interviews on my own. But I used to sleep with a Russian dictionary on my night table, because I'd lie in bed at night and think about words I'd need." And you need to understand the local culture and history, as well as the nation's traditions, in order to really succeed abroad. You also need time—time to build contacts, and time to learn the nuances of the story. Foreign reporting isn't for everyone, but if you can do it, it can be a great way to move up the career ladder fast.

It can get awfully frustrating at times in journalism. It can be hard to get yourself noticed, hard to get promoted, and hard to get good assignments. In a bad economy, it can even be hard to get a job. We've both had times in our careers when we did a job we didn't particularly like, or found it difficult to move up the career ladder. It took Mike several decades to go from being an announcer at a small radio station in Grand Rapids, Michigan, to being a star on CBS. In the end, you need to focus on building experience and expertise, and trust that the knowledge you're acquiring will ultimately pay off in your career.

It's not enough to say you want
serious news, you have to watch it.
—AARON BROWN, journalist and professor

Immortal Rules for Success in Journalism

For all the problems and challenges we've cited in this chapter, we continue to have faith in one principle: *there will always be a need for great journalism.* And no matter what the industry becomes in the next years and decades, reporters who can produce great journalism—reports with both dramatic heat and informational light—will be successful. With that in mind, let's bring things full circle and remind you of what it takes to do journalism right.

1. Break news. "The great journalists are the ones who uncover stories, who make news," Chris Wallace explains. "They are able to uncover some story that people don't want out there, who are able to break through the talking points in interviews and get people to say things they didn't intend to say when they came in." He says that's what's going on in his mind every time he anchors *Fox News Sunday.* When he's on the air, Wallace is trying to get his interview subjects to say something that will create news that day and in the following morning's newspapers. But he doesn't judge his success just by headlines or by ratings. It's also about breaking news that will impact viewers. "I think you want to add value to their knowledge, to their lives. You want to give them an understanding, a perspective on an issue that's of interest and perhaps of direct importance to their lives, that they didn't have going in," he explains. So focus on going where others have not gone—don't just repeat what everyone else is doing.

2. Go out and report. Great reporters go out of their way to find great stories. "You can only do so much reporting in your office, on your phone," says Robert Anderson. "It takes getting out there and, if you go out there, you will be rewarded with finding and coming across things that you wouldn't have come across from your phone line. As you're reporting, get the hell out of your office." It may be time-consuming, difficult, and at times exhausting to be an active reporter, but coming up with a great story makes it all worthwhile.

3. Be bold. When you're going in search of stories, address the hard subjects head-on. Be brave. "Put yourself in places you never thought you'd see," advises Michael Bronner. "Don't ask, just go—or if you have to ask, go in with good ammunition and convince the gatekeepers that the world will be well served by your gaining access—and then serve the world with the access you gain." Many of the best reporters we know are quick to take risks but also know when to bail out because the risks have become too great. Being bold also means being relentless in your pursuit of a story. When faced with adversity, a truly relentless reporter goes for the story another way instead of being put off.

4. Use your comparative advantage. Whatever you do, strive to do it better than anyone else. Learn a subject well and make that your specialty. Add value where others have not. Consider the network evening news shows, for example. "They have to cope with the fact that by the time the six-thirty news comes on, most of America has had the chance to watch the news over and over again on all kinds of channels—cable channels and, of course, the Internet," says Mike. He says that means they have to do something different to succeed—to provide the in-depth analysis that other outlets lack and to use their deep pockets to fund great enterprise reporting. Doing something different is key in a highly competitive world.

5. Work hard. "If you were to ask me what is the single greatest attribute that defines and distinguishes people who are successful from people who aren't successful, it would not be intelligence," says Chris Wallace. "It would be energy." The people who have gone far in this business tend to be extremely hard workers. It's not just about the hours. It's about putting in more effort than your competitors. "Just work harder than anybody else," advises Wallace. "Be more professional. Do your job more thoroughly. Look for different angles or different ways to pursue your job. It's the old cliché about the harder I work, the luckier I get. So many of the stories that I've gotten, the big interviews that I've been able to book, the fact that I've been able to bring out in reporting or in a question, is because I did just that extra bit of work."

6. Have patience. You don't get to be an anchor overnight. You don't win a Pulitzer or an Emmy every time you think you've worked hard enough to deserve one. "The rhythm today is one of the pursuit of instant stardom, instant million-dollar salaries, instant glory," says Marvin Kalb. "The idea of working your way up to that, even if it took ten or twenty years, produces impatience and irritation." Remember that most journalists take decades to make it. Pay your dues, serve your apprenticeship, and realize that it takes time to develop all your skills. And remember, too, that journalism, like any other business, is not always a meritocracy. Sometimes people will get promoted over you even though you think you're a better reporter. In television especially, things such as good looks and youth can lead to advancement. At CBS News, Lara Logan essentially leapfrogged correspondents with decades more experience when she was named chief foreign correspondent for the network a few years back, and that bruised some egos. These things happen. When they do, gripe for a moment and then move on. Hard work, smarts, and a good attitude do eventually bring notice. And don't be scared off by the current tough job market. "There's always going to be a hunger in our society for quality journalism," says Jill Abramson of the *New York Times*. "There's no stopping a young person with fire in their belly for the kind of work we do."

7. Never forget that it's really about other people. Approach your work with compassion and respect for the people you interview. Learn from them, and let your life be enriched by them. "Embrace people, win their trust, listen carefully to them, and find the wisdom in what they're telling you," advises Michael Bronner. Meeting people you would never get to know otherwise is the best part of being a journalist. Always be aware of the feelings of those you cover, who may be experiencing emotions ranging from great joy to great loss. Never forget that you are a human being first and a journalist second.

8. Be a team player. Journalism is not usually a solo sport. Mike is the first to admit that his success resulted from the efforts of hundreds if not thousands of people with whom he had the privilege of working. Without the help of Ted Yates in particular, who came up with the concept for Mike's breakthrough show, *Night Beat,* Mike's career in news might never have flourished. So when you're working, try to involve everyone's best talents, which almost always leads to a better product.

And don't forget that you are part of the larger brotherhood and sisterhood of journalists, and that your behavior reflects on the whole profession. Believe it or not, being a journalist sometimes means that you may even aid your competitors. Out in the field, journalists almost always help one another out by answering a question, sharing information, or lending equipment. Always try to help, even if the person who needs help is a competitor. Next time, *you* may be the one who needs help.

9. Be skeptical but not cynical. Don't believe everything you're told or everything you read—believe things after they've met your own personal test for veracity. Go into things with an open mind, and follow the evidence and facts to their logical conclusions. Treat government officials with special skepticism. That's your job as a journalist. "Journalism is never aggressive enough, never bores in enough, and that's one thing that young people need to know. They need to know to never take yes for an answer and to never fall for what the government is telling them or what a company is telling them or what anyone's telling them," says Pelley. "Spinning the news has been done for thousands of years, but I think in this day and time, with the Internet and the blog world, that it gets done a lot more. And there's a huge tidal wave of spun information that is flowing over us all the time. And young reporters need to get old-fashioned and get down into the roots of the information. Get multiple sources, and make sure you're talking to original sources, the people who really have their hands on the information."

10. Don't get a big head. The news business is filled with people with large egos. This is something to be avoided at all costs. Russ Mitchell, who is often complimented by his colleagues for staying especially down-to-earth, says he has seen journalists who have somehow lost themselves. "This is something I've always wanted to do, to work in broadcasting and to be a broadcast journalist," he says. "It's a great job—but at the end of the day, it's a job. When you leave the job, you're who you are. Hopefully, the job doesn't change who you are." So our advice is to stay humble. Everyone loves working with people who are low-maintenance. Despite the rigors of your job, try to have a full life outside of the office, and have fun with what you do. "This is a profession that really is full of fun—the joy of the chase, and the sort of wonder and satisfaction that comes from being able to sift through your reporting and tell a story really beautifully," says Abramson.

11. Find yourself a moral compass. Marvin Kalb says that when he started working at CBS News, he used Edward R. Murrow as a check on his actions and reporting. "Would Murrow approve?" Kalb says he asked himself. "I'd never want Murrow to be disappointed. And that says something." But Kalb says it's different today. "I'm not sure there's a Murrow there today that stands as a guidepost for young journalists. I don't know that they think that if they do something wrong that someone is going to be terribly disappointed," he says. "That's a big, big loss." So find a person who can serve as your personal moral compass. It could be a family member, it could be an editor or producer, or it could even be a legendary figure of journalism such as Edward R. Murrow. It's better if it is a living person, one to whom you can actually turn for advice and guidance. The point is to find your bearings and to aim high.

12. Remember, the world is counting on you. If journalists do not uncover evil and injustice, who will? Even in this wired world, we still need people who will dig below the surface to expose wrongdoing and hold people responsible. "The quality of life in America is dependent on the quality of the journalism," says Scott Pelley. "Most people don't realize that, but if you think about it, journalism is one of the pillars on which our society is perched. And you can't pull that pillar out. It relates to the quality of our politics, it relates to the quality of life, it is essential to having a great country." This is the most essential function of journalism, the heart of everything we have tried to teach you here.

So if that's the kind of journalism you want to do, you now have the basic knowledge to start working. Now go out and conquer.

Reporters' Toolbox

1. Checklists

Print Checklist

- Did I spell everything here correctly?
- Did I use punctuation correctly?
- Did I check my publication's stylebook to make sure I used words correctly?
- Is my lede clear and powerful?
- In my hard news story, after I read the first two or three paragraphs, do I know what the story is about?
- In my hard news story, have I gotten the most important points of the story into the first two or three paragraphs?
- Did I write my hard news story in the inverted pyramid style, with the most important information at the beginning of the story?
- Did I put a direct quote in paragraphs 3, 4, or 5 of the story? If not, would that make the story stronger?
- Did my direct quotes add emotion, humor, or color?
- Did I read my story through for logic?
- Did I check the spelling of all names?

- Did I check the titles for everyone in my story?
- Did I double-check all my facts?
- Did I double-check to make sure that my quotes are completely accurate?
- Have I assumed anything in my story that may not be true?
- Does my article sound like something from a newspaper, or does it feel like an essay or term paper?
- Did I keep my sentences short and clear?
- Did I keep my paragraphs relatively short?
- Did I omit needless words?
- Did I use the active voice?
- Did I inject my opinion into the article?
- Did I use judgmental words in the article?
- Have I been fair to the people I interviewed?
- Have I explained the essence of the story fairly and in a balanced way?

Radio Checklist

- Is the story clear, and does it cover the most important material?
- Did I use natural sound as well as people speaking?
- Do the sounds I use help tell the story?
- Did I record those sounds at the place where I reported? If not, they probably don't belong there.
- Did my best sounds and best sound bites make it into the piece?
- Did I create word pictures of the things my audience cannot see?
- Is my lede short and punchy?
- Will my lede hook the audience?
- Did I write into each sound bite effectively?

- Did my direct quotes add emotion, humor, or color?
- Did I introduce the speaker before each sound bite (or immediately after, if I used a short bit before a longer quote)?
- Did I mention each person's title on first reference?
- Did I refer to each speaker properly on second and later references?
- Did I check the titles for everyone in my story?
- Did I read my story through for logic?
- Does my story have an appropriate ending?
- Did I double-check all my facts?
- Did I double-check to make sure that my quotes are completely in context?
- Have I assumed anything in my story that may not be true?
- Did I keep my sentences short and clear?
- Did I omit needless words?
- Did I use the active voice?
- Did I inject my opinion into the story?
- Did I use judgmental words in the story?
- Have I been fair to the people I interviewed?
- Have I explained the essence of the story fairly and in a balanced way?
- Did I read in an upbeat but unrushed tempo, punching the most important words?

Television Checklist

- Is the story clear, and does it cover the most important material?
- Do the words and pictures in my story match?
- Did the words I use add to the pictures instead of repeating what can be seen?
- Did my best pictures, best sounds, and best sound bites make it into the piece?

- Is my lede short and punchy?
- Will my lede hook the audience?
- Did I write into each sound bite effectively?
- Did my direct quotes add emotion, humor, or color?
- Does my story have a standup that adds credibility?
- Did I read my story through for logic?
- Did I check the spelling of all names and make sure they're correct in any supers?
- Did I check the titles for everyone in my story?
- Did I mention every quoted person's title, either in the text or in the super?
- Did I refer to each speaker properly on second and later references?
- Did I double-check all my facts?
- Did I double-check to make sure that my quotes are completely in context?
- Does my story have an appropriate ending?
- Have I assumed anything in my story that may not be true?
- Did I keep my sentences short and clear?
- Did I omit needless words?
- Did I use the active voice?
- Did I inject my opinion into the story?
- Did I use judgmental words in the story?
- Have I been fair to the people I interviewed?
- Have I explained the essence of the story fairly and in a balanced way?
- Did I read in an upbeat but unrushed tempo, punching the most important words?

Internet Checklist

In addition to the Print Checklist, use this list when writing for the Internet.

- Can I create graphics, interactive or noninteractive, that will add to the overall reporting?
- Can I add a print article to my site?
- Can I add a television story?
- Can I add a radio story?
- Can I add a podcast?
- Can I add a slide show?
- Can I add a timeline?
- Can I add personal stories in some way?
- Can I add links to other sites on this subject that might be helpful to my audience?
- Can my audience comment or add information to the site?

2. TV Script Formats and Sample Broadcast Script

Here is how you actually write out a television script:

A. The narration usually goes in ALL CAPS, to help correspondents who may have to read a script off a BlackBerry or other PDA see the text easily. The sound bites go in caps and smalls.

B. The pictures that you plan to show go in parentheses above the text they will cover, like this:

(put what the pictures show in parentheses)
TRACK: HERE IS WHERE THE NARRATION GOES.

C. Start your script with a *slug*, which is one or two words summarizing what the story is about. Below that, put the show, date, and name of correspondent (and producer and editor if there is one).

D. When you have a sound bite, write down the information for the super, including the person's name and title, and put the full text of what that person says. Remember that the super may not be able to include someone's full title or where they work.

SUPER: Name and title of person speaking
SOT (Sound on Tape): Exact text of the quote

Here's an example of how it all fits together:

SAMPLE SCRIPT

U2
Smith/Jones/Baker (correspondent/producer/editor)
Evening News 3/6/10 (the show where the report will appear, and the date)

(U2 in concert, sound up, sings the song "Beautiful Day")
TRACK 1: ROCK SUPERSTARS DON'T USUALLY PLAY COLLEGE CAMPUSES, ESPECIALLY NOT AT THE BREAK OF DAWN.

(cu Bono)
TRACK 2: BUT U2 ROCKED FORDHAM UNIVERSITY IN THE BRONX TODAY, IN AN EARLY MORNING CONCERT AIRED LIVE ON ABC'S *GOOD MORNING AMERICA*.

SUPER: Bono, lead singer, U2
SOT Bono: "We joined a rock-and-roll band to get out of going to college, but maybe if it looked like this, things could have been different."

(more band plays)
TRACK 3: IT WAS SUPPOSED TO BE A SECRET CONCERT—PART OF THE BAND'S PUBLICITY TOUR FOR ITS NEW ALBUM, *NO LINE ON THE HORIZON*.

(students jump up and down to music)
TRACK 4: BUT WORD GOT OUT, AND THOUSANDS OF FORDHAM

UNIVERSITY STUDENTS SPENT ALL NIGHT IN LINE, TO GET A GOOD SPOT.

SUPER: Christopher Rodgers, Dean of Students, Fordham University
SOT RODGERS: "We tried to keep it secret because we were afraid of being overrun by U2 fans. For security reasons, the concert was only open to students and alumni."

(more U2 playing)
TRACK 5: BUT MORE THAN FOUR MILLION VIEWERS CAUGHT THE CONCERT ON TV. THE BAND'S TRYING TO SELL ITS NEW ALBUM, AND ALSO FILL STADIUMS AROUND THE COUNTRY AS IT SETS OUT ON A NEW TOUR.

STANDUP, NEAR STAGE WITH BAND AND STUDENTS BEHIND
"This concert caps off a busy week for the band. They hung out with the mayor, appeared each night on David Letterman's show, and even got a street named after them in midtown Manhattan."

(Band sings, sound up: "Hello, hello . . ." from the song "Vertigo")
TRACK 6: THE BAND PLAYED SIX SONGS, THEN STUCK AROUND TO SHAKE HANDS AND SIGN AUTOGRAPHS.

SUPER: Bono, lead singer, U2
"This is exactly where we come from. Not from the Bronx, but we started our band when we were seventeen and eighteen. This is our home."

(Setup shot, Jennifer Sawyer dancing)
TRACK 7: AND FORDHAM STUDENTS SAID THAT THEY WERE HAPPY TO SHARE THEIR HOME WITH THE FOURSOME FROM DUBLIN.

SUPER: Jennifer Sawyer, Fordham Student

SOT Sawyer: "This was the best concert I've ever seen. I was up all night to get a good position, but it was so worth it! I love U2!"

(Song ends, the band members start waving to audience)
TRACK 8: AND FROM NOW ON, THANKS TO U2, FORDHAM MAY BE KNOWN AS THE SCHOOL OF ROCK.

3. Structure for a Basic 1:30 Broadcast Piece

Remember that your piece must answer all eight basic questions of journalism (who, what, when, where, why, how, so what, what's next).

Also choose five points that you want to make in the piece, and put them in order—then incorporate them into the narrative.

(Start with your best pictures)
LEDE that hooks you. May or may not make one of your five central points. Should be short and punchy.
Narration—making at least one or two of the five central points in your piece.
Lead-in to first sound bite

SOUND BITE 1
More narration—making at least one of the five central points in your piece.
Lead-in to sound bite two

SOUND BITE 2
Yet more narration—making at least one of the five central points in your piece.
Possible standup for television feature piece
Lead-in to sound bite three

SOUND BITE 3
Concluding information—including any of the five central points that you have not yet made.

(second strongest pictures, or logical ending pictures)

End—conclusion, end of story, feeling of closure. Possible standup if television news piece.

4. Glossary of Terms in Journalism

Beauty shot A shot in a television report that is particularly striking.

Bite Sound bite, a person talking.

B-roll Assorted generic shots.

Checkbook journalism Paying someone in return for an interview.

Chyron The information written on the screen, such as a person's name and position. Same as **super.**

Clip A sound bite.

Close When a reporter returns to the screen, usually after a taped report.

Closed-ended question A question that requires a simple yes or no.

Close-up Close shot focusing on something small. Same as **tight shot.**

Crawl The words that scroll across the bottom of the screen on some news shows.

Cut In editing, the change in a shot.

Cutaway A shot to be used in editing where the camera shoots something other than the main action, like a correspondent listening. A cutaway is useful in editing.

Desk Organizational parts of a news operation (e.g., national desk, foreign desk).

Direct lede Hard news lede that contains specific information about what happened.

Direct quotes Quotations using a source's exact words.

Elements Different elements in a story (e.g., the people to be interviewed, places to shoot).

Enterprise reporting Original reporting, often based on inquiry or investigation.

Feature A soft news story; a topical story that is not required to run on a particular day.

Get The big interview of the day that every journalist is trying to secure.

Hard news News that is breaking.

Indirect lede A beginning of an article that does not immediately reveal what the story will be about. Often an anecdote or story. Also called a delayed lede.

Insert A taped report that is partnered with a live introduction and/or close.

Inverted pyramid Ordering facts in a hard news story from most important to least important.

Kit A cameraperson's gear.

Lede The first line or two of an article or broadcast script.

Libel tourism Suing an author for libel in another country where libel laws are weaker than in the author's home nation.

Live shot A television report where the correspondent appears live, usually at the scene of news.

Medium shot A shot that is neither wide nor close. It may show one or two people or a small area.

MOS Man on the street; sound from a random person. Same as **vox pops.**

Moving down Moving something in a story closer to the end.

Moving up Moving something in a story closer to the beginning.

Natural sound (NATSOT) Sound that is not from an interview. May be naturally occurring or mechanical.

News peg A piece of news that can be linked to a feature story, giving the feature a timely aspect.

Nut graph Paragraph that summarizes the significance or main theme of a feature story.

On-cam Reporter appears on camera to say something. Same as **standup.**

Open The beginning of a live report.

Open-ended question A question that cannot be answered with a simple yes or no.

Package A taped television report, edited and with narration.

Pan Moving camera shot from side to side or up and down.

Pitch To propose a story.

Pull Moving camera shot going from close to wide.

Punching Emphasizing words as you read a broadcast script.

Push Moving camera shot going from wide to close.

Rundown List of reports that will appear in a broadcast.

Setup Shots of people being interviewed showing them doing something.

Signoff The reporter's identification at the end of a story.

Slug A one-word summary of what your story is about.

Sock puppeting Pretending to be a reader and making an online comment about a story you yourself have written.

SOT Sound on tape. Same as **sound bite.**

Sound bite A quotation. Same as **bite.**

Sound up Natural sound that gets louder and then recedes under the narration of a report.

Staging Causing an event or getting someone to do something for the cameras.

Standup Reporter appears on camera to say something. Same as **on-cam.**

Super The information written on the screen, such as a person's name and position. Same as **chyron.**

Talking head A person in a report who says something without much action.

Tease The words that tell viewers what will be coming up later in a news show.

Throw Ask a person to talk (at end of report, correspondent usually throws to anchor).

Tight shot Close-up.

Track (n.) The correspondent's voice or narration, which carries through a report; (v.) to record the correspondent's voice for a television or radio report.

Voice-over (V/O) A voice, usually the anchor's, over pictures.

Vox pop Interview with a regular person or bystander. Same as **MOS.**

Wallpaper Pictures that cover text but don't really tell the story.

White balance A measurement taken by a television camera to make sure the picture is exposed properly.

Wide shot A shot that shows a lot of a particular scene.

Zoom in Same as **push.**

Zoom out Same as **pull.**

5. To Go Further . . .

Here are some activities to help you dig deeper into the lessons of each chapter.

Chapter 1

Watch Mike Wallace's interview with Ayatollah Khomeini, at www.cbsnews.com/video/watch/?id=4455573n. Ask yourself whether Wallace was after heat or light.

Read Edward R. Murrow's 1958 speech to the Radio and Television News Directors Association. Was he right about the future of television? Debate whether journalists should or can remain completely neutral.

Watch one hour of CBS News, Fox News Channel, and MSNBC. Ask yourself how much of each network's reporting is in the objective style and how much is opinion-based. Which style do you prefer? Why?

Read the policies on social networking at news organizations such as the *New York Times*, the Associated Press, and the *Wall Street Journal*. Do you think they are fair?

The *New York Times* policy: www.poynter.org/content/content_view.asp?id=157136

The AP policy: www.wired.com/images_blogs/threatlevel/2009/06/facebookfollow/

The *Wall Street Journal* policy: www.laobserved.com/archive/2009/05/wsj_staffers_told_to_be_n.php

Imagine what you would do if your requests for a formal interview with someone were turned down. When would you resort to an ambush interview, and when would you just look for someone else to interview?

Watch, listen to, or read a news report. Ask yourself what elements of it relate to our definition of heat, and which to light.

Chapter 2

Watch an episode of *60 Minutes* and ask yourself how the correspondent and producers may have come up with the ideas for the stories. Try to come up with a good idea for a *60 Minutes* story on your own.

Watch or listen to a journalist renowned for doing interviews. It might be someone at *60 Minutes*, Terry Gross of National Public Radio's *Fresh Air*, Bill Moyers of PBS, Barbara Walters of ABC, or someone on a local station. Analyze the questions asked. How many of them seemed written in advance, and how many were follow-ups to something the interviewee said? Did the questions become more difficult as the interview went on? What in the interview showed that the interviewer did his or her homework?

Imagine you've been given the chance to interview your favorite actor. Ask yourself how you would go about doing the research necessary for a good interview. Write ten questions you would ask this star, and put them into some logical order.

Watch a Sunday morning political talk show. Ask yourself how the anchor makes the discussion understandable to a wide range of Americans while also trying to break new ground. How many of the questions seem to be written in advance and how many are follow-ups? How did the anchor reflect his or her background research in his questions?

Look at some of the ambush interviews on *The O'Reilly Factor* on Fox News, or in any of Michael Moore's movies, such as *Roger and Me* or *Bowling for Columbine*. Ask yourself whether they contained light (information) or just heat (drama).

Chapter 3

Watch some of Mike's interviews on the Internet. Ask yourself questions about his interviewing style. How does it vary from interview to interview? How does he establish rapport? How does he phrase his questions?

Watch interviews by the likes of Ted Koppel, Barbara Walters, Ed Bradley, Bill Moyers, Chris Wallace, or Jon Stewart. Or listen to the masterly Terry Gross on her public radio show *Fresh Air*. How do their styles vary? What techniques do they use to establish rapport? How does doing a live interview differ from doing a taped interview? Ask yourself: does a reporter's gender or race make a difference?

Read an interview transcript done by a reporter for a major newspaper or news magazine. There are interviews printed in full all the time. Evaluate the reporter's style and technique. Ask yourself if he or she might have done something differently had the report been done for broadcast.

Watch Chris Wallace's September 26, 2006, interview with President Bill Clinton on the Internet or read the transcript. Ask yourself how you might handle an interview that turns contentious.

Interview the oldest members of your family about its history and traditions.

Chapter 4

Take a hard news article from your local newspaper. Analyze it to see whether it is written in the inverted pyramid style.

Take two hard news articles from your newspaper and apply the First Five formula. Which elements are contained in the reports' first five paragraphs? Do they fit the First Five formula? How?

Find a feature story in a magazine or newspaper. What kind of lede does it have? Does it hook you? How is the story organized?

Find a hard news story with a hard news lede, and a hard news story with a feature (indirect) lede. Which one hooks you more quickly?

Pick a newspaper or magazine story and see how the author writes lead-ins to quotes. See how the quotes are attributed. Can you find the print triad of lead-in, quote, and attribution?

Sign on to the Pulitzer Prize website at www.pulitzer.org and read some of the winning entries. Take special notice of the lede, the structure, and the quality of the writing.

Chapter 5

Watch a news broadcast, national or local. Pay attention to how the words and pictures work together. How do they add to one another? When do you just see wallpaper?

Listen to one of National Public Radio's main news shows, either *Morning Edition* or *All Things Considered.* Listen for stories that use natural sound. How does the sound add to the narration and sound bites?

Watch some reports by one of our favorites, the late, great Charles Kuralt of CBS News, and analyze how he writes his stories about average Americans. Several of his pieces are at www.cbsnews.com, on YouTube, or available on DVD. How does he fashion a lede? How does he get your attention? What clever words does he use? How does he incorporate natural sound, pictures, and sound bites? What makes his pieces so good? Then compare his work to a CBS correspondent today who does the same kind of stories, Steve Hartman. There are dozens of his pieces at www.cbsnews.com.

Look at some standups on a news show. Were they in the middle or at the end of the piece? Where were they shot? What kinds of things did the reporter say? How much was analysis? How much was a description of something for which there was no video? How did having a standup add to the piece?

Look over the website for the PBS documentary *Bush's War* at www.pbs.org/wgbh/pages/frontline/bushswar. Look through the interviews and other resources posted on the Web and ask what value all this material has to the average viewer.

Pick front-page articles from your local newspaper and conceive of additional elements you could add online.

Chapter 6

Indiana University has a wonderful website that deals with ethical issues. The site has a few dozen cases of real-life ethical dilemmas, and each one explains how the real reporter in question resolved the dilemma. Sign on and read a few. Do you agree with how the reporter reacted? See journalism.indiana.edu/resources/ethics.

The Society of Professional Journalists has links to the Codes of Conduct for a few dozen organizations on its website. Read through some of these Codes. How are they the same? How do they differ? See www.spj.org/ethicscode-other.asp.

Look up some of the central Supreme Court cases of media law at www.oyez.org. Read through them. What do they say about the reasons to have a free and active press?

Check to see if your state has a shield law. If it does, try to find the law and read it, to ascertain your right to keep the names of sources confidential. See Reporters Committee for Freedom of the Press, Privilege Compendium, at www.rcfp.org/privilege.

Chapter 7

Read the latest "State of the News Media" report from the Project for Excellence in Journalism at www.journalism.org. Ask yourself what is new in the news business.

Check out the winners of some of journalism's top awards: the Pulitzer Prizes, the George Polk Awards, the News and Documentary Emmy Awards, the Overseas Press Club Awards, the Alfred I. DuPont–Columbia University Awards, the National Magazine Awards, the Edward R. Murrow Awards, and the Sigma Delta Chi Awards. Many of the award websites let you read the winning stories or see the winning entries. Take some time to go through the winners. See who won, and ask yourself why they might have won. See "Journalism Resources" later in Reporters' Toolbox for addresses.

Explore the awards and fellowships available to young journalists. These include the Rolling Stone Annual College Journalism Competition, the Livingston Awards for Young Journalists, the Robert F. Kennedy Journalism Awards, and the Evert Clark/Seth Payne Award for Young Science Journalists. There are many more awards than these, which you can find online. See if something you have done or something you might do could be entered. See "Journalism Resources" for addresses.

If you're a college journalist, join the Associated Collegiate Press; if you're in high school, join the National Scholastic Press Association. Both these organizations hold conventions, give awards, and provide useful training to young reporters. See www.studentpress.org for both organizations.

Get in the habit of reading the websites that deal with the media business. Some of our favorites are the Poynter Institute website and its column of daily news compiled by Jim Romenesko (www.poynter.org), MediaBistro (www.mediabistro.com) and its associated sites, and the *Columbia Journalism Review* (www.cjr.org) and *American Journalism Review* (www.ajr.org) sites. The Monday business section of the *New York Times* also usually contains a few stories on the news media.

6. Journalism Resources

See our website, www.heatandlight.org, for a full list of online resources. Join our Facebook group, Heat and Light, for updates.

General

Committee to Protect Journalists—www.cpj.org
Investigative Reporters and Editors—www.IRE.org
Media Bistro—www.mediabistro.com
National Press Club—npc.press.org

Newseum—www.newseum.org
Pew Research Center's Project for Excellence in Journalism—www.journalism.org
Poynter Institute—www.poynter.org
Reporters Without Borders/Reporters Sans Frontieres—www.rsf.org
Society of Professional Journalists—www.spj.org

For Student Journalists

Associated Collegiate Press—www.studentpress.org
CNN Student News—www.cnn.com/studentnews
Columbia Scholastic Press Association—www.columbia.edu/cu/cspa
Investigative Reporters and Editors student page—www.ire.org/education/highschools.html
Journalism Education Association—www.jea.org
National Scholastic Press Association—www.studentpress.org
New York Times Campus Weblines—www.nytimes.com/learning/general/specials/weblines/index.html
Quill and Scroll International Honor Society for high school students—www.uiowa.edu/~quill-sc
Student Press Law Center—splc.org

For Your Career

JOBS IN JOURNALISM

Editor and Publisher—www.mediajobmarket.com
Jobs in Journalism, University of California at Berkeley Graduate School of Journalism—journalism.berkeley.edu/jobs
Journalism Jobs—www.journalismjobs.com
Journalism Next—www.journalismnext.com
Media Bistro—www.mediabistro.com

Pew Center, Project for Excellence in Journalism, Job Resources—www.journalism.org/resources/job_links

TRAINING AND FELLOWSHIPS

American Press Institute—www.americanpressinstitute.org

Fellowship, Scholarship and Grants Database, American Journalism Review—www.ajr.org/awards1.asp?awtype=1

Joan Shorenstein Center on the Press, Politics and Public Policy, Harvard University—www.shorensteincenter.org

John S. Knight Fellowships for Professional Journalists, Stanford University—knight.stanford.edu

Knight-Bagehot Fellowship in Economics and Business Journalism, Columbia University—www.journalism.columbia.edu/knight-bagehot

Knight Digital Media Center, a partnership between the University of Southern California Annenberg School of Communications and the University of California at Berkeley's Graduate School of Journalism—www.knightdigitalmediacenter.org

Knight Science Journalism Fellowship at MIT—web.mit.edu/knight-science

Knight-Wallace Fellows—www.mjfellows.org

Nieman Foundation—www.nieman.harvard.edu

Maynard Institute—www.mije.org

Poynter Institute—www.poynter.org

PRIZES

Alfred I. DuPont–Columbia University Awards—www.journalism.columbia.edu

Awards Database, American Journalism Review—www.ajr.org/awards1.asp?awtype=1

Edward R. Murrow Awards, Radio and Television Digital News Association—www.rtdna.org/pages/awards.php?g=67

Emmy Awards, National Academy of Television Arts and Sciences—www.emmyonline.org

Evert Clark/Seth Payne Award for Young Science Journalists—www.mindspring.com/~us009848

George Foster Peabody Awards, University of Georgia—www.peabody.uga.edu

George Polk Awards, Long Island University—www.brooklyn.liu.edu/polk

Goldsmith Awards, Harvard University—www.hks.harvard.edu/presspol/prizes_lectures/goldsmith_awards

Livingston Awards for Young Journalists—www.livawards.org

National Journalism Awards, Scripps Howard Foundation—www.scripps.com/foundation/programs/nja/nja.html

Overseas Press Club Awards—www.opcofamerica.org

Pulitzer Prizes, Columbia University—www.pulitzer.org

Robert F. Kennedy Journalism Awards—www.rfkmemorial.org/legacyinaction/journalismawards

Rolling Stone Annual College Journalism Competition—www.rollingstone.com/journalismcontest

Sigma Delta Chi Awards, Society of Professional Journalists—www.spj.org/a-sdx.asp

For Industry News and Information

MEDIA NEWS

Daily Briefing, Pew Research Center's Project for Excellence in Journalism—www.journalism.org/dailybriefings

Media Bistro—www.mediabistro.com

NewsHour with Jim Lehrer, PBS, Topic: Media—www.pbs.org/newshour/topic/media

On the Media, National Public Radio—www.onthemedia.org

Reliable Sources, CNN, transcripts—
transcripts.cnn.com/TRANSCRIPTS/rs.html
Romenesko's Media News, Poynter Institute—
www.poynter.org/column.asp?id=45

PUBLICATIONS

American Journalism Review—www.ajr.org
American Society of Newspaper Editors High School Journalism Project—www.highschooljournalism.org
Columbia Journalism Review—www.cjr.org
Editor and Publisher—www.editorandpublisher.com
Nieman Reports—www.nieman.harvard.edu/reports
Quill, Society of Professional Journalists—
www.spj.org/quill.asp
TV Quarterly—www.tvquarterly.com

MULTIMEDIA/ONLINE JOURNALISM RESOURCES

Cyberjournalist—www.cyberjournalist.net
Digital News Journalist, City University of New York Graduate School of Journalism—digitalnewsjournalist.com
J-lab, the Institute for Interactive Journalism—www.j-lab.org
Knight Digital Media Center, with terrific tutorials on how to use software such as Audacity, Garage Band, and Final Cut Pro—
multimedia.journalism.berkeley.edu/tutorials
Online Journalism Review—www.ojr.org
Online News Association—journalists.org

For Writing a Story

REPORTING RESOURCES

Citizen Journalism Toolbox, ePluribus Media—
discuss.epluribusmedia.net/cjtoolbox
Database Library, Investigative Reporters and Editors—
data.nicar.org/node/61

Fed Stats, government website with links to federally gathered statistics—www.fedstats.gov

A Journalist's Guide to the Internet, a wonderful site run by Christopher Callahan, dean of the Walter Cronkite School of Journalism at Arizona State University—reporter.asu.edu

Power Reporting, a site by Bill Dedman with hundreds of useful links—www.powerreporting.com

Reporter's Tools, *American Journalism Review*—www.ajr.org/news_wire_services.asp?mediatype=13

Reporter's Toolbox, Knight Center for Environmental Reporting—ej.msu.edu/resources.php

Reporter's Toolbox, American Press Association/Illinois Press Association Foundation—illinoispress.org/index.php?option=com_content&view=article&id=50&Itemid=70

Reporter's Toolbox, Society of Professional Journalists—www.journaliststoolbox.org

FREE PRESS/FREEDOM OF SPEECH

American Civil Liberties Union—www.aclu.org

First Amendment Center—www.firstamendmentcenter.org

National Freedom of Information Coalition—www.nfoic.org

Oyez Project, with Supreme Court cases, arguments and analysis—www.oyez.org

Reporters Committee for Freedom of the Press—www.rcfp.org

Student Press Law Center—www.splc.org

GOVERNMENT ORGANIZATIONS

Census Bureau—www.census.gov

Federal Communication Commission—www.fcc.gov

Government Printing Office, a rich site with databases for searching for laws and government documents—www.gpoaccess.gov

U.S. House of Representatives—www.house.gov

U.S. President—www.whitehouse.gov

U.S. Senate—www.senate.gov

U.S. Supreme Court—www.supremecourtus.gov

JOURNALISM RESEARCH ORGANIZATIONS

Accuracy in Media—www.aim.org

American Press Institute—www.americanpressinstitute.org

Annenberg Washington Center—www.annenberg.northwestern.edu

Association for Education in Journalism and Mass Communication—www.aejmc.org

Center for Investigative Reporting—www.centerforinvestigativereporting.org

Center for Media and Democracy—www.prwatch.org

Center for Media and Public Affairs, George Mason University—www.cmpa.com

Dart Center for Media and Trauma, University of Washington—www.dartcenter.org

European Journalism Centre, in English—www.ejc.net

Fairness and Accuracy in Reporting—www.fair.org

Freedom Forum—www.freedomforum.org

Joan Shorenstein Center on the Press, Politics and Public Policy, Harvard University—www.shorensteincenter.org

John S. and James L. Knight Foundation—www.knightfoundation.org

Media Matters for America—www.mediamatters.org

Media Research Center—www.mediaresearch.org

Pew Research Center for the People and the Press—people-press.org

Tyndall Report—tyndallreport.com

PUBLIC ACCESS TO INFORMATION

Reporters Committee for Freedom of the Press, letter generator for Freedom of Information Act requests—www.rcfp.org/foialetter

Reporters Committee for Freedom of the Press, Open Government Guide with rules for each state's open records and open meetings laws—www.rcfp.org/ogg/index.php

Search Systems, for searching public documents—www.searchsystems.net

Student Press Law Center, letter generator for making public records requests—www.splc.org/foiletter

Journalism Groups and Associations

PRINT

American Press Institute—www.americanpressinstitute.org

American Society of Magazine Editors—www.magazine.org

American Society of Newspaper Editors—www.asne.org

Newspaper Association of America—www.naa.org

Newspaper database from American Journalism Review—www.ajr.org/newspapers.asp?mediatype=1

BROADCASTING

National Association of Broadcasters—www.nab.org

NBC Icue, a learning environment based on NBC News archives—www.icue.com

Radio and Television Digital News Association (RTDNA)—www.rtdna.org

BEATS

Association of Health Care Journalists—www.ahcj.umn.edu

Center for Science and Medical Journalism—www.bu.edu/com/jo/science

Education Writers Association—www.ewa.org

Military Reporters and Editors—www.militaryreporters.org

National Association of Science Writers—www.nasw.org

Religion Newswriters Association—www.rna.org

Society of American Business Editors and Writers—sabew.org
Society of Environmental Journalists—www.sej.org

DEMOGRAPHIC

Asian American Journalists Association—www.aaja.org
Association for Women in Communications—www.womcom.org
Association of Young Journalists and Writers—www.ayjw.org
National Association of Black Journalists—www.nabj.org
National Association of Hispanic Journalists—www.nahj.org
National Lesbian and Gay Journalists Association—www.nlgja.org
Native American Journalists Association—www.naja.com
South Asian Journalists Association—www.saja.org

Contributors

Abramson, Jill, managing editor, *New York Times*

Anderson, Robert, producer, CBS News, *60 Minutes*

Blum, Ron, sports reporter, Associated Press

Brauchli, Marcus, executive editor, *Washington Post*

Bronner, Michael, contributor, *Vanity Fair*

Burton, Eve, general counsel, Hearst Corporation

Chivers, Christopher, correspondent, *New York Times*, and contributing editor, *Esquire* and *Field & Stream*

Ford, James, reporter, WPIX-TV, New York

Garlick, Lin, executive editor, CBS Newspath

Hayes, Arthur, associate professor of communication and media studies, Fordham University

Hickey, Neil, professor of journalism, Columbia University Graduate School of Journalism, and former New York bureau chief, *TV Guide*

Hopp, Neil, director of student publications, Central Michigan University

Kalb, Marvin, professor emeritus, Harvard University, John F. Kennedy School of Government, and former correspondent for CBS News and NBC News

Keller, Bill, executive editor, *New York Times*

Marshall, Joshua Micah, founder and editor in chief, Talking Points Memo

Mason, Linda, senior vice president, standards and special projects, CBS News

Mitchell, Russ, anchor, *The CBS Sunday Night News with Russ Mitchell*

Murphy, Kim, correspondent, *Los Angeles Times*

Palmer, Elizabeth, London correspondent, CBS News

Pelley, Scott, correspondent, CBS News, *60 Minutes*

Ramirez, Anthony, former reporter and editor, *New York Times* and *Fortune*

Scanlon, Chip, instructor, Poynter Institute

Smith, Robert, correspondent, National Public Radio

Wallace, Chris, host, Fox News Channel, *Fox News Sunday*

Acknowledgments

First of all, we would like to thank all the people who spoke with us for this book. Some interrupted their vacations to speak with us; others wrote us long e-mails from assignments halfway around the world. Their contributions have made *Heat and Light* far more useful, interesting, and enlightening than we could have made it alone. Heartfelt thanks to you all.

Thanks next to Mike's assistants: Rachael Kun, Barbara Neil, and Pam Carelli. Thanks also to Peter Olberg, who dealt with all the legal issues and was greatly helpful in nudging the book toward completion.

Thanks to some other people who assisted with setting up interviews for the book: Carolina Valencia of the *New York Times*, Heidi McCormick, Cynthia Knapp of the Hearst Corporation, Michele Keleman and Anna Christopher of National Public Radio, and Ed Prewitt.

We gratefully acknowledge the support of CBS News in the preparation of this book. Special thanks to Linda Mason, senior vice president, and Robert Anderson, Mike's longtime producer at *60 Minutes*, for giving so graciously of their time and being early supporters of this book. The traditions of CBS News are in our bones, and we are both proud to be part of the "Tiffany network."

Beth also wants to thank the former staff of the CBS News Moscow bureau for providing a home away from home.

Beth feels extremely lucky to serve on the faculty of Fordham University, and to enjoy the support of a superb group of colleagues. She is particularly indebted to the former chairman of the Department of Communication and Media Studies, Paul Levinson, and the current chair, James VanOosting, for their enthusiastic support of this work, and to Professor Arthur Hayes for checking the section on media law.

Beth would like to thank a few close friends who lent their support during this project: Torrey Clark, Lisa and Arieh Coll, Diego Diaz, Joseph DiVito, Jennifer Eremeeva, Roberta Faulk, Herade Feist, Richard Froehlich, Ira Gilbert, Susan Jane Gilman, Jonathan Gray, Robert Pastore, Jonathan Sanders, Sushma Soni, Myrna Tarter, Charles Valade, James and Alicia Weinstein, and Priscilla Vazquez. Thanks to a few mentors: Michael Parks, John-Thor Dahlberg, Richard Boudreaux, Richard Threlkeld, and David Hawkins. Thanks to you Facebook friends, too, and to my students for the constant flow of encouragement. Special thanks to Mark Shulman, assistant dean of the Pace University School of Law, for reading the manuscript. Thanks also to Beth's family for their constant love and support: Matthew Knobel, David and Trish Knobel, Mark and Raquel Knobel; the Davis, Friedland, and Schenker families; the whole Fells family; and Tamara, Stanislav, and Gleb Belyaninov. And Beth thanks her husband, Kirill, and son, Alexander, for their love, support, and patience through all these months.

We also thank our two wonderful research assistants on the book, Fordham graduates Emily Scharnhorst and Meredith Engel, for their hard work on the manuscript. Thanks also to Sue Warga for copyediting the book.

Very special thanks to Chris Wallace, for finding the time—despite his incredibly busy schedule—to read and critique the manuscript.

Special thanks as well to our agent, Doug Grad. We feel incredibly lucky that Doug started his own literary agency just when we needed an agent for *Heat and Light*. His wisdom has infused what we have written here, and the book is far better for his having been a part of it.

This book would never have happened without the fabulous Julian Pavia, our editor at Crown. He has been another champion of this work, who from moment one has been totally on our wavelength about what it should be and how it might help the profession. He is wise beyond his years, and his thoughtful edits and sound advice improved this work vastly. Thank you, Julian. You're phenomenal.

And there is one person without whom this work really would have never happened: Mary Yates Wallace, who supported this book wholeheartedly from the moment of its inception. Beautiful, charming, adventurous, and nurturing, Mary has a spirit that inspires everyone around her. We hope that we have written a book here that will make her proud.

Index